AUTHOR'S NOTE:

Fair warning, the topics covered in this book are basic and more likely to help those just starting out on their publishing journey, rather than experienced authors.

Other titles by
Danielle Ackley-McPhail

THE ETERNAL CYCLE SERIES
Yesterday's Dreams
Tomorrow's Memories
Today's Promise

THE ETERNAL WANDERINGS SERIES
Eternal Wanderings

THE BAD-ASS FAERIE TALE SERIES
The Halfling's Court
The Redcap's Queen
The High King's Fool
(forthcoming)

Baba Ali and the Clockwork Djinn
(with Day Al-Mohamed)

The Literary Handyman
Build-A-Book Workshop
More Tips From the Handyman

The Ginger KICK! Cookbook

SHORT FICTION
A Legacy of Stars
Transcendence
Consigned to the Sea
Flash in the Can
The Fox's Fire
The Kindly One
Dawns a New Day
The Die Is Cast
(with Mike McPhail)

The Literary Handyman
Tips on Writing From Someone Who's Been There

Danielle Ackley-McPhail
with an introduction by Ty Drago

Pennsville, NJ

PUBLISHED BY
Paper Phoenix Press
A division of eSpec Books
PO Box 242
Pennsville, NJ 08070
www.especbooks.com

Copyright © 2011, 2018 Danielle Ackley-McPhail

ISBN: 978-1-942990-65-9
ISBN (ebook): 978-1-942990-66-6

All rights reserved. No part of the contents of this book may be reproduced or transmitted in any form or by any means without the written permission of the publisher.

"A Little Friendly Abuse" originally published as "Where Two, or Three, Or Twenty Are Gathered" in The Complete Fantasy Writer's Guide Volume Three: The Author's Grimoire, edited by Valerie Griswold-Ford and Lai Zhao, published by Dragon Moon Press, 2007.

"The Naming of Names", "The Tricky Art of Conversation", "Continuing the Conversation", and "Wrapping Up the Conversation" originally published under the ongoing column The Writer's Toolbox, in Allegory Magazine.

Interior Design: Danielle McPhail
Cover Design: Mike McPhail, McP Digital Graphics
Cover Art: Bryan Prindiville, http://www.bryanprindiville.com

Dedication

To an awful lot of people who paid it both forward and back
along this journey of mine, including:
L. Jagi Lamplighter,
Jeffrey Lyman,
Lee C. Hillman,
David Goldstein
CJ Henderson,
Bernie Mojzes,
Ty Drago,
and all of my Yesterday's Dreamers

And especially for Mike, for giving up my time.

Contents

It's Not Brain Surgery 1
A Word Before We Get Started 3

Craft

On Being Inspired 7
Put a Little Magic into It 11
Soul Food: Feeding Your Passion 15
Establishing Reality in Your Fantasy 17
The Naming of Names 21
Populating Worlds 29
So You Think You Know... 37
The Tricky Art of Conversation 41
Continuing the Conversation 47
Wrapping Up the Conversation 53
Spending Your Words Wisely 59
Literary Detailing 63
Coming to Your Senses 67
The Short and the Long of a Novel Idea 73

Writing Exercises 77

Business

Always Another Day Away 95
In Godhood Is Perfection Found 101
Flexibility Is a Virtue 105
Rejection and the Tender-Hearted Youth 109
A Little Friendly Abuse 113
Anthologies 125
On the Sizes of Fishes and Ponds 131
Something More Than a Thick Skin 137
Promoting For the Beginner 145
General Publishing Terms 149
Summing Up 153
Ty Drago 155
Danielle Ackley-McPhail 157

It's Not Brain Surgery

There's a relatively famous anecdote about writing, one that has been ascribed to everyone from Stephen King to the late John D. MacDonald, author of the Travis McGee mysteries. It goes something like this:

A writer and a brain surgeon are at a party and start talking about what each other does for a living. The brain surgeon says to the writer, "You know, I've always wanted to be a writer. I think I'll start tomorrow." The writer replies, "Really? I've always wanted to be a brain surgeon. I think I'll start tomorrow."

The point, of course, is that wanting to be a writer and *being* a writer are two very different things. I respectfully disagree and, in fact, tell the same story a bit differently:

A writer is approached at a party by a woman who says wistfully, "Oh! You're a writer! I've always wanted to be a writer." And, to this, the writer replies, "Really? I've always wanted to be a brain surgeon."

My humble though adversarial point is that if you want to be a writer, you write. There's no other requirement, a fact that simply doesn't apply to most other avocations. For example, it isn't a very practical approach to brain surgery. Nevertheless, the very moment you put pen to paper (or words on a computer monitor) for no reason other than the desire to communicate with your fellow human beings, you are a writer.

Congratulations!

Now becoming a *good* writer; that's something else altogether.

Once you've committed yourself to authorship, where do you start? How do you find inspiration? How should your story be told? What sort of characters do you need to create in order to populate what sort of world? And once you have your finished tale, how should you market it? What happens when it's accepted or — more likely for new writers — when it's *not*?

The Literary Handyman addresses these questions, and more.

Writing is a craft, like knitting or gardening. A person can, to some extent, be taught to write. All it takes is time, patience, and barrels full of practice. It also helps more than a little bit to have the advice of someone who's been there.

In November of 2009, Danielle first approached me with her idea of authoring a series of short essays on writing for my online fiction magazine *Allegory*. Her first such article, entitled "The Naming of Names" appeared in our Winter 2009 issue under the banner *The Writer's Toolbox*. That essay can be found in this volume, among her many others.

The reader response to her *Allegory* debut was so positive that I immediately reached out to Danielle for more, and she's since been our first ever non-staff columnist. Given the success of *The Writer's Toolbox*, when she later proposed compiling her work into *The Literary Handyman*, I was naturally excited at the prospect, and honored when she asked me to write the introduction.

Within these pages, Danielle's take on the craft of writing is intelligent, insightful, and often quite funny — as is the woman, herself. She tackles, with style and skill, everything from the mysteries of dialogue to the vagaries of the modern publishing world.

There's a good deal to be gleaned here. My advice is read it, enjoy it, and most importantly, use it. The path of a serious writer is lonely and often arduous. There's a lot to learn and a lot to do along the way.

And a literary handyman is — well — *handy*.

Ty Drago
Author, Editor, and Publisher

A Word Before We Get Started

First off... no... I'm not a guy, but *The Literary Handywoman* just didn't have the same charm.

Second off... this is and has always been a beginner's guide. If you are already established as an author this is all going to be basic knowledge for you.

Now... on to what I wanted to say!

Have you ever opened a toolbox? An honest-to-goodness working toolbox? No, I'm not talking about one owned by an obsessive-compulsive where everything is locked down and labeled. I mean just your everyday, jumbled collection of tools like most of us have somewhere in our homes. Yeah, that's the one... you open it up and have to paw through it to find precisely the right tool, but you know it's in there because this is a good handyman's toolbox.

Well, that's what I hope you'll find in this book. I'm less concerned with order and structure and everything in its place, this isn't a college course, after all. (Though to be honest, even if it was, I'd likely still do it my way.) Don't look for a step-by-step guide or an intensive refresher course on grammar and structure (those are out there in more than sufficient quantity already, and even if they weren't, I don't feel I'm the one to tackle explaining the English language).

No, I'm not teaching you how to be writers because frankly, everyone's process is different. Besides, if you have picked up this book it is likely you already *are* a writer. The rest comes with experience.

What I want to give you are the tools—the knowledge I have learned and the advice I have been given—for you to adapt in a manner that most benefits your growth as a writer. This is my effort to help you build that publishing career you are after (though I do recommend you consider it more of a serious hobby... there is less frustration that way) without imposing my own view of what that should be.

In *The Literary Handyman* you will discover a collection of mostly stand-alone articles. Some of them are brand new, others are recycled from either my column *If We'd Words Enough and Time* (from the defunct website www.fictionauts.com), or my column *The Writers' Toolbox* (previously featured in the online magazine *Allegory*, www.allegoryezine.com.) Since they were all written at different times and for different purposes I ask your patience as there will surely be some points that are repeated. That said, I like to think that much of what is here bears repeating, which is why they haven't been rewritten for the purpose of this handbook.

When all is said and done, these articles draw on my experience of over twenty years as a publishing professional, over fifteen of which I have also been a published author. Being a genre author, some of that will be evident in my examples, but for the most part the advice in these pages is not specific to genre writers. It is my hope that whatever you are inspired to write, you will benefit from what I have learned on my singular, ongoing journey.

Dream Big!

Danielle Ackley-McPhail

Craft

On Being Inspired

You know, there will be many people out there who will raise their voices in outrage at what I'm about to write.

So... are you ready for it?

Writers don't have to write every day to be writers.

No, really. This is not grounds for my turning in my union card. If you subscribe to the philosophy that you do need to write something every day, that is all well and good. I'm glad if it works for you and yes, one would hope by doing so you will hone your skills and produce both quality and quantity. For me, though, I just don't have the time. Now, that doesn't mean I am not a serious writer. To the contrary, I have six published novels to my name and countless short stories and articles that have seen print. (You can find a listing of these at the back of this book.) Of course, I've been doing this for a long time.

This does not mean that I don't *encourage* writers to write every day, just that I acknowledge that it isn't always practical, given the hectic schedules and volume of responsibilities that are common to each of us in today's society. That is why I am talking about this here and now, the very first thing, because I don't want anyone out there to feel they are somehow lacking because they can't dedicate some portion of time to their craft *every* day. I don't want any writers out there to be discouraged or feel they are anything less than what they are because they can't meet this dictate.

Now that I have made that clear, let's look at ways to get yourself writing when you do have time!

Being Practical

You've all had those times when you are not inspired or can't find the next thread in the story you are working on. I know you have. There isn't one of us that hasn't had a moment like that. There are ways around it, and sometimes they even work. Here are a few I've tried with some measure of success.

Polishing. If I can't make any progress writing new material, I force myself to start reading the piece from the beginning, correcting and tweaking as I go along. Occasionally, by the time I reach the end I am ready to pick up where I left off. This isn't precisely writing in that it doesn't always generate much in the way of new copy, but it does help me polish what I've already gotten down so I don't have to spend as much time cleaning up the story or novel later. Of course, if you feel you work better getting everything down first before you can edit, this may not be an option, in which case I have a few other suggestions.

Immersion. This can help with productivity, though not always. Remove distractions so that you don't have any option but to write. Put yourself in a secluded space, (or put a "do not disturb" sign on the door and flip the lock), put on some mood music (without words, I would recommend, unless that type of thing doesn't distract you), and make sure you have a snack and plenty to drink at hand. Now for this to work you need to make sure your computer is not a source of distraction on its own. For me, I had to remove all of the games that came pre-loaded and I have to stay disconnected from the internet, though that isn't always an option when I know I'll need to do research.

Multitasking. No, not quite in the traditional sense, but when I can't make headway on one project, I jump to another. This isn't always an option for everyone, but if you are like me and have three or four pieces going at once it can work. When I hit a stumbling block, it helps if I'm able to get somewhere on a different piece.

Assignments. If your goal is just to write, rather than to write on a dedicated project, get someone to give you an assignment or a challenge. Alternatives would be to set one for yourself, or to find a contest or submission opportunity on line and use the designated theme as your assignment. I find this helps when you aren't motivated because so many of us grew up used to English assignments. In some ways it is more comfortable and easier to mimic that experience because you have a focus and a deadline, rather than having to find the motivation from within yourself. This also has the added benefit of giving you a potential home for whatever you write. Joining a writer's group would be a similar incentive to be productive.

The Uncomfortable Truth

Nothing is going to work one hundred percent of the time. And if you force yourself, who is to say that the end product is going to be worth the effort? I am sure, as with myself, there are days where you are just totally unmotivated or incapable of writing. The trick is to let those happen. If you aren't geared up to write, forcing yourself isn't always going to have the effect you want, though sometimes it does work. If my literary neurons aren't firing, I crochet and watch movies, or if I really want to be totally unproductive and veg, I read a book from dawn until dusk... okay... midnight and beyond, but what is your point? Sometimes we need that decompression time... a reminder that life is more than work and a computer screen. This should be something you enjoy in life, not something that takes you away from it.

Put A Little Magic Into It

(Originally published in The Broad Sheet, the newsletter of the international organization, Broad Universe.)

The world is full of wonder. Sometimes we forget that. Everything that happens contains a little bit of magic or miracle. As writers, particularly genre writers, we need to focus on that.

One of my favorite things is to take an event… just a normal event, and put a twist on it. Think what would make it different. An early example of this, in my eighth grade English class we had to write a story. My story was about the splendor of a moonrise, so overlooked and underappreciated in comparison to the sunrise. Now that is unusual in itself.

My narrator… a rubber band dropped in a garden.

What can I say; I've always been odd that way.

Writers are in a unique position where they get to reorder the readers' perception of the world. Give them rules and a framework for understanding and you can do anything you imagine. One way to do this is to create a social structure of knowledge for your characters. Think out the hows and whys and what-fors. Just remember, even with fantasy, logic has to be in there somewhere, or you better be prepared to explain why it isn't. Once you have that in place you can play in the new reality you've created exploring character dynamics and heroic challenges with your imagination as the guiding force. Nothing to hold you back but yourself. This can be a lot of work, but also a lot of fun for the author. Kind of like the first time you received a box of crayons…

at first you were a two-year-old Jackson Pollock, then as you gained control and understanding, a recognizable order began to take shape. First squiggles corresponded with the rough area on the page where they belonged, then a little while later you understood the concept of coloring within the lines, until ultimately you learned the joy of telling the lines to take a flying leap and made your own image.

In the speculative genres, we only have the lines we impose on ourselves.

One of the ways I like to explore this open field is to take the tropes everyone is familiar with and rearrange them. Currently I'm playing in the faerie realm. The twist: *my* faeries are bikers. Now, I know most people will say "What the heck?" But my bikers are modeled on the concept of faeries that kept generations of villagers leaving offerings on their hearths and hanging scissors over their babies' cradles. Old World faeries had teeth... and worse. They were tough and harsh and malevolent. They were warriors. I mingled a bit of the old-world with the new, channeled magic into wings of energy and introduced the peculiar nature of the biker culture, complete with legends of their own, to revitalize the Disney-fied fae.

There is so much of world myth that has been lost to common knowledge, but not lost to time. A little bit of exploration on the internet or at your local library and you can find so many forgotten treasures to revamp your speculative playground.

A good example of this are vampires. Yes, everyone has their own concept... from the Anita Blake novels to Sookie Stackhouse and beyond. But how much of what you read is modern invention of pop culture and how much is based on an actual existing myth? You would be surprised about how much of what everyone "knows" about vampires just from the Stoker novel is unsubstantiated by the actual legends found in nearly every culture. I have done research on vampires around the world for a current—unconventional—vampire novel I am working on and discovered only one legend that actually credits their version of vampires with not being able to go into the sun. If you want to explore an overdone subgenre do a little research, draw on uncommon knowledge about the common populous of our paranormal world... and if there is something so entrenched the readership will be in an uproar if you try and mess with it... rearrange what you cannot change.

One of my favorite things to do is find or devise an unanticipated reason for the assumptions everyone makes about a myth cycle. Just as an example, most elf or faerie fiction will claim that these creatures covet human young because they do not have many of their own. And why don't they have many of their own? It is popular belief that immortal (or near immortal) beings do not have the same need... compulsion... to reproduce as energetically. Since they live so long they don't need to worry about replacing themselves before it is too late... basically. For me, I wanted a different reason, one that had at least the illusion of being grounded in the existing mythology. My elves rarely have young because the Irish believe in reincarnation, but they believe that you come back as your descendants. With that in mind, in my novels, *Yesterday's Dreams* and *Tomorrow's Memories*, which are based on Irish mythology, the elves are incapable of having young unless one of them dies... because that frees up the soul to return. Finite amount of souls, death equals birth. That gives me some implication that there is a mythological basis.

I like to play that way. There is so much that you can do out of your own imagination or by exploring the underutilized aspects of existing mythology that can breathe new life into the speculative genres, setting your work apart from the cookie-cutter books that invariably begin to surface with the popularity of any particular trend in fiction.

Play, have fun, don't tie yourself down to what everyone *expects*. Above all, create.

Soul Food
Feeding Your Passion

(Originally published in the column If We'd Words Enough and Time)

Popcorn is nothing more than a butter vehicle. Let me say that again... popcorn is nothing more than a butter vehicle.

What the heck?! Right?

Now I'm sure your "What the heck?!" has completely different connotations from mine, so let's take a moment to explore them both: now my explanative was a shocked response, a spontaneous and completely understandable reaction to the blasphemy I myself have dared to utter. Popcorn, that light, airy manna, nothing more than a vehicle for something else? Those who know me can well understand my shock.

Here comes the surprise part: the blasphemy, for me, is true. Popcorn has absolutely no appeal for me dry. (Trust me, I am going somewhere with this.)

Shall we now examine your "What the heck?!"? That would be the "What the heck does this have to do with writing?!," right? Well I'm sorry, but it has everything to do with writing — once you stop to realize the written word is our popcorn.

Come on, don't walk away now... I know you're dying to find out where I'm going with this. You've come this far already...

In life, as in our writing, there are things that exist merely as a means to savor that which we love. Commercials exist so we can get our snacks; popcorn and crusty Italian bread exist so we can indulge in creamy butter; stale, near-tasteless tortilla chips are merely a means of getting flaming salsa to our tongues;

fights break out so that we can console ourselves with chocolate… you get the idea.

Well, when we write, our words exist so that we can write about what we love (such as buttered popcorn… I LOVE buttered popcorn) It is important to remember this—the part about the writing, not the popcorn—Words are our passion vehicle.

What is your passion? For me it is the richness of myth, an intricately woven tale full of hidden significance and vibrant descriptions. I love deep, evocative emotion and personal triumphs over adversity… not the kind that are handed to you on a platter, but the kind that required clawing and struggling and life-transforming decisions to obtain. I like poetry that is in your face and on your sleeve. And, if you couldn't tell, I like my nonfiction witty (I can only hope) and a little bit cheeky.

Now I know there is writing that pays the bills and writing that feeds your soul, and you might find yourself in a position where you must divide your time among both of them, but do not allow what you are required to do to crowd out what you are driven to do. Find the time to nurture your own creativity. If you are fortunate enough to have a choice in the bill-paying variety of writing, write what interests you, but even if you can't, be sure that you invest yourself in your words, let them carry your passion for all things, for only then will they be heard.

Remember, when we write, it reflects our beliefs, our interests, our souls. A piece of ourselves is left forever on the page, so make sure that what you leave behind is true to who you are, what you want the world to see. So, whatever you must write, for personal gratification or personal survival; find a way to make it yours. Turn everyone's expectations on their figurative ear and make your words a vehicle for whatever it is you need to say, what you believe in.

If you are not passionate about what you are writing, whether it be fiction, nonfiction, or poetry, then what is the point? Write first for yourself and only then can you speak to the masses.

Establishing Reality In Your Fantasy

I know... I know... seems like I'm contradicting myself, doesn't it? Not really. No matter what you are writing—science fiction, fantasy, romance, etc.—you need to establish some reality that your audience can identify with. Sometimes this draws on your own experience (after all, mostly we do write about what we know), but sometimes we want to explore something different. For my novel, *The Halfling's Court: A Bad-Ass Faerie Tale*, I wanted the backdrop of a biker bar with my primary character the leader of a biker gang. I am not a biker. I don't interact with bikers. I've only been on a motorcycle once.

Yeah... what was I thinking! Actually, I was thinking this is going to be really cool! It was also a lot of work, though. See, bikers aren't just tough men and women (or faeries, in the case of my novel) wearing leather and riding motor bikes. There is an entire culture there, right down to a unique language that to the uninitiated definitely needs translation. Fortunately for me, there are a lot of biker sites out there that have glossaries of terms that define the phrases for you and even put them into context. This was invaluable to me when I went to incorporate flavor into my story. Some of it was obvious and I could just substitute the terms for other words I would generally use, for example:

"What'll you have?" asked the hot, young mattress cover masquerading as a waitress.

But often I had to work a bit of explanation into the text. Case in point:

"You keep tellin' yourself that," she murmured, her gaze brutal in its wisdom. "These riders are here to make the run with you... with the Wind Walker."

He hissed through clenched teeth. "Anyone can be a wind walker; all it takes is treating people right, looking out for them on the road."

It was a challenge to insert just enough "color" without alienating the reader. I sprinkled in some motorcycle and biker facts, used the language where it felt appropriate and not forced and then let the story progress. It took research, but with the internet there is more than enough material out there on virtually anything you could want to use as a theme. And for what is not readily accessible, consider interviewing someone living in that culture or take a field trip (if that is an option) to observe people similar to the characters you wish to write. For me it was simple. My main character, Lance, is physically based on my uncle, and the secondary character Bubba is based on my brother. I have first-hand experience with their personalities and mindset as it applies to the culture I wanted to portray.

Once I had the biker elements incorporated I could work in the fantasy thread I needed for the story, in fact, in a way this was simpler than if I had chosen a different social group because believe it or not there are already fantasy elements in the biker world. Primary for my purposes was the legend of the road gremlin. See, the original biker gangs were made up of retired Air Force personnel. In the Air Force if something went wrong with a plane it was gremlins. When they transitioned into bikers that bit of legend came with them, morphed into road gremlins. To protect themselves from this hazard bikers hang little bells off their motorcycles. The ringing either scares the gremlins away from the bike before they get on, or it traps them in the bowl of the bell if they are already in residence. This was an ideal element for me to incorporate to link "reality" with "fantasy."

To further strengthen the link between my bikers and the magical realm of faeries my biker gang is called the Wild Hunt, mirroring the legendary Hunt found in myth and folklore, only substituting motorcycles for the horses the faeries would ride. Also to mirror the magical realm the hierarchy of a biker club mimics a Court (as in royal or faerie) structure, thus setting up the primary conflict in my tale.

When I applied magic to my characters it was something appropriate to their lifestyle… helmets spelled for protection, magic tattoos that link one character with another… things you would expect in real life, only with a magic twist.

After all, that is the challenge. Give a reader just enough that is familiar to them and then give it an unexpected twist. Now this context is urban fantasy, but a similar foundation can be applied to high fantasy equally as well. Just take the culture or social group you want to emulate and do your research, then find ways to adapt their identifying features to a fantasy setting.

Have fun, play with it, but definitely do your homework because if you don't capture the proper feel it doesn't matter how well written the other aspects of your story are, if one thing doesn't ring true it throws off the whole story.

The Naming of Names

(Originally published in Allegory Magazine, www.allegoryezine.com)

Have you realized how much a name can say about someone? Well, maybe not so much today, where the blending of culture and celebrity and downright boredom has led to some combinations that simply ignore things like tradition, religious/ethnic background, and even gender. But at one time you had a good chance of telling where a person was from, their sex, their occupation, and sometimes even roughly when they were born just by learning their name. Some places in the world you still can.

Our challenge as writers is to match that rich process. Parents on average name one, two, or at most a bare handful of children in their lifetime. Authors populate worlds. Now, not every character needs a name with layers of meaning. Many won't even need a name at all, but when the name does count, how do you go about finding or creating one?

Good question! Let's talk…

The Don'ts

First off, let's get some basics out of the way. There are a few things that you want to avoid when naming your characters. After all, you want them to complement your story, not detract from it.

Don't Get Cute. Unless there is a specific reason for it, such as you are writing a children's story or pulp fiction, try to avoid names that sound like they are the butt of a bad joke, like Hope

Bright or Candy Kane. Do it too often, or without a relevant reason, and you'll just make it harder for the reader to take your character—and your story—seriously.

Don't Be Difficult. Names have a structure we are familiar with. Even if it's in another language, we can generally recognize the pattern of a name. A well-constructed one is comfortable to say, as well as to hear (unless, of course, the voice is your mother's and she's using all three of yours at once).

Now this is mostly for those writing fantasy or science fiction, but if you are creating a name for an alien or non-human race, have mercy on your reader and try and mirror the above-mentioned pattern. For example, in the movie *The Fifth Element*, the perfect being had a name about thirty syllables long... for effect. It was quickly shortened to the more manageable and name-like Lelu.

Don't Echo. What do I mean by that? When you have a number of characters involved in a storyline, it is important that the reader be able to easily distinguish which character you are talking about at any given time. This need increases exponentially the more characters that are involved. So, even though in life it is quite common for people to at least partially share the same name or similar sounding names, you absolutely do not want your characters to do so—unless, of course, there is a very good reason for it that is integral to the plot. Mike and Ike makes for a catchy name for a candy, but have such a duo in a story and you could easily leave your reader confused when things really get going. Less common, but also something you should watch out for is having a character and a race, city, or other story element with similar sounding names. Like using Vargas from Vegas, this could be a rather unfortunate combination.

Don't Mirror Life. Unless you are writing historic fiction or your story has a specific need to include or allude to a figure from recorded history or current events, be careful of using name combinations for characters that mirror those of notable people that actually exist or did exist at one time when you aren't actually writing about that individual. Also be careful of mirroring the names of other distinct fictional characters. In extreme cases of either example, it could lead to accusations of libel or copyright violation, and possible legal action against you. (For the same reason, some in the industry often caution against using the name or representation of someone you know even with their permission, because it has been known to occasionally be poorly received. This, of course, is a personal choice you must make.)

The Do's

Once you are ready to actually get down to naming your characters there are a lot of things to consider, questions to ask yourself as you establish their persona, and steps you can take to ensure you have the right one. For our current purposes, let's assume you have already chosen your character's name.

Do Confirm. As I mentioned, sometimes a character's name will have some particular relevance—as with Harry Copperfield Blackstone Dresden, from Jim Butcher's *Dresden Files*, a wizard named after three of the world's greatest magicians—and sometimes it will just be something to identify who is who, but in either case run a web search on it once you have chosen. I recommend you look for several things: Are there any negative associations with real-life individuals? Does the (first) name have a meaning that is unfortunate, inapplicable, or perhaps apropos? Has a similar or identical name been used for a character in someone else's book? (With everyday kind of names, this isn't really an issue, but if the book is of a similar type to what you are writing, or if there are parallels in the plot or character development, they could be used to substantiate an accusation of plagiarism, such as in the case with Disney's Simba and the story of Kimba the White Lion. The best you could hope for in such situations is to be accused of a lack of originality. At the worst you will be looking for a lawyer.)

Do Be Consistent. Make sure your character's name is both spelled and used consistently throughout. Settle on the different variations you might use for formal and informal encounters, any titles, ranks, or honorifics, and do not vary from what you have established. An exception to this would be if your character has a particular nemesis or bully that uses an incorrect or ill-preferred variant of the name to annoy said character, or a friend or family member that can't or won't use the more common variant, but without malice.

Do Be Appropriate. Make sure you select a name in keeping with the time, setting, and social position of the character, where applicable. Also, make sure supporting characters have names that complement one another and work together to establish your environment. After all, having a character from a primitive tribe deep in the Brazilian rainforest named Charles isn't really going to be plausible (Unless, of course, you build some justification into the story).

The How-To's

Some people are good at picking names. Some agonize over it. I find if you have a method, it goes a lot simpler, and the joy: you aren't limited to just one! On those occasions where the name doesn't just come to me I have plenty of tricks for picking one out. Here are a few of them.

Morality Play Method. It was standard in these medieval works to name a character after the predominant trait they represented, such as Charity, Hope, Avarice, etc. That lacks a certain subtlety for modern works, except for the rare virtues that are accepted as names today. However, I still like the idea of this method, but with a twist. I write a lot of fantasy, usually mythology based; for those characters that I wish to use the MP method of naming I go to the language associated with whatever myth cycle I am using. For example, my first novel, *Yesterday's Dreams*, is based on Irish mythology. I wanted to name my antagonist Evil so I looked up the word in my Irish-English dictionary. Several different words were listed so I chose to go with "Olcas" because it seemed the most like an actual name. By an ironic twist, when I was later doing research into the mythology I ran across a rather nasty fellow from the actual legends named Olcas and I was able to adapt my plot to that myth rather nicely.

Defining Characteristics. A variant of the above, only the name represents a notable physical trait, rather than just the more usual virtues. An example would be my character Kerwin. When he first appeared in the short story "At the Crossroads" he was introduced as the Dubh Fae, Irish for the black fae. This had a dual purpose because he was dark in coloring and nature. When that story was expanded into my novel, *The Halfling's Court*, he needed a true name. It also turned out that he was an outcast among his own kind, shunned because of his dark, crude features. To that end he gained the name Kerwin, which means the little black one, in this case an insult to a grown fae.

Historic/Cultural Relevance. Depending on what type of story you are writing it might be applicable (as in the aforementioned *Dresden* reference) to add layers of meaning to your work by borrowing all or part of a name from the history books or newspapers. This is a little different than what I describe above in the "Don'ts" section. Do so with care. I tend to use this more for naming vessels or installations than people in my science fiction, and when I use it in my fantasy I'm more likely to borrow the name of an applicable mythological personage, than I am someone that actually lived. For example, I have a character that insisted on the nickname Scotch no matter how I tried to change it. I didn't discover the reason for the nickname until I'd written three more stories using the character… he was apparently Corporal Jack(son) Daniels, (thus the nickname Scotch) and it just hadn't come up on the page yet.

Made-up Names. For those that write fantasy or science fiction, at some point you are going to find yourself with a story where what we recognize as names just won't be applicable. You could just pick something obscure from another language, or you can make up something yourself either whole-cloth or echoing an actual name. If you do be sure to read it aloud to feel what it sounds like. Keep it simple and follow a recognizable pattern. If you start out with a complex name, be sure to establish a shorter version that will be easier on the reader when the action gets going (or yourself, should you be in a position to read your work aloud in front of an audience.) When you must make up a number of names for a common group, try to establish a unifying syntax so the reader can believe the individuals come from the same culture. Or, conversely, distinctly different syntax if the characters are from separate environments. Try to avoid apostrophes or Latin-construct endings, these have become somewhat cliché.

For Your Toolbox

To get you started on populating your worlds, here are some questions to consider in relation to the character and setting.

What time frame/setting are you writing in? Very important as in some cases this will determine if you use recognizable names or those that are made up or altered. Also, name usage changes over time, with old names falling out of favor and new ones being established. Lingual shift can even cause the spelling of established names to change, which you can use in your favor if writing a future piece.

Are there established naming protocols for this time frame? Some cultures, classes, and religions are very specific on how a child is to be named. Research some of these traditions to give a more realistic feel to your work.

What is the character's gender? Some names are clearly gender specific, while others are gender neutral. Over time, some have even switched their orientation. In some cultures names are unisex, with a change in suffix identifying gender, such as Angelo versus Angela, or Ivanov versus Ivanova. Whatever pattern you establish, remain consistent.

What is the character's social standing? While in most modern cultures names are not restricted by social class, they can be an indicator, such as the stereotypical Buffy, Muffy, and Biff of the well-to-do set, as characterized in fiction and media, or Billy-Joe-Jim-Bob and Katie Sue, for more rural individuals. Now I don't usually recommend such stereotypes, but they can be useful to quickly and cleanly establish a type of character... or turn one on its ear.

What is the character's ethnic background? Some names are specific to those of an ethnic group, or such groups have a variant of a common name, such as the Polish version of Agnes, which is Agnieszka. Be careful of using a clearly identifiable cultural name when not writing in that particular cultural setting or of choosing names from different cultures for members of the same group and assuming the reader won't notice. All they need to do is recognize one of the names to make assumptions about the characters that could be completely wrong. Not really an issue if you are writing in modern-day America, but if you are writing in a fantasy world a recognizable name could prevent the reader from immersing themselves in the created reality.

Is there a cultural/religious tradition in the naming of children? In centuries past, as in different societies today, children are named for relatives, saints, and other culturally determined conventions. This goes for surnames as well, where some children were identified by their personal name followed by their parent's name (Erikson) or occupation (Cooper).

The Summing Up

Basically, names should sound like names and they should fit your character and your story. With the advent of the internet it is relatively easy to find names from different cultures, variants on common names, and the meanings of names, not to mention historical documents such as census reports that can tell you particular names popular in a given era or region. If you are unsure, look to what exists in the world for inspiration; there are countless examples all around you!

So, with no further ado, let us commence with the naming of names!

Populating Worlds
The Imprecise Science Of Characterization

You know, as much as I have gone on about characters and those things that go into building them, I am astounded to realize that I have not, until now, written a dedicated article on creating characters. There is something wrong there. Something very wrong.

(… cue melodramatic music…)

I'm sure you want to know why, right?

Well… because I haven't had a reason to before! (I would have thought that one was simple.) Now as for why it is important to discuss character creation… that is much more complex.

Have you ever been at a party, or a function, or heck, just sitting quietly on the bus minding your own business and someone starts talking to you? Not a friend or a companion, just a stranger? Imagine they start telling you stories about themselves or people you don't know and frankly don't care about. They go on and on until your eyes want to cross and you contemplate getting off at the next stop, even though it isn't yours, just to get away from them.

Okay, maybe a little extreme, but the same thing goes for fiction. If the reader doesn't get a sense that they know the characters, they don't have a reason to care what happens to them. If they don't care, why read? If you don't catch their interest, a reader is going to just close the book and never open it up again. If you are lucky, they stop there; if not, look out for the scathing reviews.

Now… you don't want that, do you?

Didn't think so. As authors it is our job to make our characters real. And what is more, we have to make the reader care about them, even those they aren't supposed to like.

Let's take a look at how.

Putting a Face to the Name

We've already talked extensively about naming a character, so I won't go into that here, other than to say yes, they should have one. And once you have one, you should share it as soon as possible with the reader (unless, of course, there is a compelling reason to keep it to yourself for the time being.) But where do you go from there? I do a lot of gaming conventions, and not having created a game myself or been involved with a published one in any official capacity, at those conventions the only thing I can talk about as a guest panelist is—you guessed it—writing. You would be amazed at how many gamers want to be writers.

Okay... maybe not.

Anyway, the nice thing is that gamers already have plenty in common with writers. They tell stories and they create characters. They have help that writers generally don't, though. Gaming is a collaborative effort. While the players determine what their individual characters do, it is the Game Master (or GM) who is responsible for the plot and setting of the game, which is mutable depending on the choices made by the players. And when characters are generated (or rolled up) their capabilities and even some of their physical traits are dictated by the players' choices in relation to the process outlined in the game manual and the luck of the dice. (Each game is bloody different so I won't go into all of this, but trust me, I am going somewhere with it.) The game manual only takes them so far, though.

Now, as for why gamers have to roll up characters... It's a cheat sheet. By rolling up a set character before a game begins the player—and the GM—knows what that character is capable of, what they know, what they look like, and often even something of their history, depending on how in-depth the generation process is. This is important because everyone playing needs an idea of who they are dealing with.

The truth is, with gaming characters or fiction characters, the more the creator invests of themselves into the creation, the more interesting things are going to be. Even if the details don't come out right away — or even at all! — just the fact that they have been set helps make the character more real for the writer and the reader. The more you put into it at the beginning, the more everyone will get out of the experience in the end. That is one of the reasons I like to use gaming for an example because there are key points that must be filled in before the game can even be played:

Physical characteristics. This covers all of the basics: hair and eye color, age, build, height, weight, gender, and race. Sometimes there is more, sometimes less, but these are pretty standard. In gaming, most of this is just to get the player into the swing of things and so the GM can describe the characters to the other players when called for during the course of the game. It makes things more real. Don't forget things like scars, physical condition, and manner of dress. In fiction these details are vital for establishing the visual of the character in the reader's mind, as well as their personality. In addition to appearance, some traits determine what a character is physically capable of doing.

Learned skills. In gaming, when you roll up a character their abilities are dictated by the choices the player makes and the physical characteristics they either chose or which are determined by the roll of the dice. For example, if a gaming character has a "strength" rating of forty out of a possible one hundred — just saying — then they aren't going to be a broad-sword-wielding barbarian. And a female warrior with a charisma rating of three isn't going to be a beauty queen in her spare time.

Writers don't have those same restrictions. They get to choose what suits the purpose of the story and then it is their job to make it work. For them, characters can be or do anything, as long as the writer sets things up appropriately to make the claims plausible in the reader's mind. (Yes, that having been said, not all writers bother with the whole making it plausible bit... but frankly, do you want to be that kind of writer?) As writers you should have some basic idea of the specialized skills your character may need based on what that character is and what they are going to face. You can't anticipate everything, don't even try... and don't worry about it when something comes up that you didn't plan for; that is what revisions are for. It is important, though, not to give your character skills on the fly. Either establish that they learned certain things earlier, or actually have them go through the process of learning the new skill needed during the course of the story. You also don't want to claim abilities for them which your earlier description of them implies would be contrary to their nature. (Kind of like the examples in the first paragraph of this section only you are restricted by your own choices and not the luck of the dice.)

Personality traits. Some things will either naturally develop, or even change as you progress through your story, but some things are basic. Is your character a bore? Do they have an insecurity complex? Are they overly proud? Are they extremely nurturing or sneaky? You want to get an idea of this before you even start because the character's verbal and physical responses need to ring true. Actions and reactions are dependent upon personality and morality. If you don't set the guidelines the character will do so on their own and not always in a beneficial way. I know when I was writing my first novel my main character had a bad habit of being whiny in her dialogue throughout the first draft. Besides making her unsympathetic and annoying, it was contrary to what I had established for her in the narrative. It also set her up as a weak character, which was okay in the beginning of the book, but needed to change radically by the end. Needless to say I had to go back and revise. By learning who the character is before you sit down to write you can head off such problems because it makes you more aware of how actions and dialogue relates to "who" that character is.

Flaws. Yes, I said flaws. Imperfections. Weaknesses. Interpersonal kryptonite. Physical handicaps. Everyone has them so don't make your characters perfect. Readers can't identify with perfect because *no one* has ever seen it in our lifetime. Flaws make characters more real, but in addition to that, flaws give them something to overcome (or for another character to exploit.) Such things are vital for advancing a plot and for bringing life to a story. To go back to my original gaming example, this is one of the reasons players roll for various attributes. The dice cannot be predicted and by using them the players introduce challenges to their characters that they then must work around or with to achieve their goals. (So in a way, writing is role-playing for one.)

Personal/family history. As individuals we interact with the world not only based on who and what we are, but also based on what has happened to us or those around us. It's called experience. Everyone has it. Your characters should as well. History is what drives our reactions; it is those layers of detail that give life depth. Know why your characters say and do the things they do. Understanding where a character comes from is as important to a reader, often, as seeing where they are going. Think of such details as threads in a tapestry. The thread is pretty in and of itself, but when you weave them together they form a rich image that is much more than the sum of its parts.

Environmental influences. We are all products of our environment. Culture, society, home life, politics, all of this affects our views and responses to different situations. Characters should be the same way. Think of the different racial, religious, and cultural stereotypes you are familiar with; sad to say, but they are stereotypes for a reason. When you place a character in a particular setting it will impact the way they talk, think, and act. These are learned behaviors. If your character has learned something different than his peers, you as the writer need to account for why. Whether your character adheres to the typecasts or is contrary to it, be mindful of the reader's expectations based on the information you have given them.

The Voices in Your Head

Listen. Your characters are there. Get to know them before you attempt to tell their tale. Know what to expect from them the way you would with a good partner, one you know well enough to anticipate their responses. This isn't to say that characters won't do things that surprise you. Things that are... forgive me... out of character, but as with all of us, there are reasons, you just have to figure out what they are.

Questions to Ask Yourself

Here are just a few things for you to think about while developing your characters. Not all of them will apply in every instance, but by applying some of the below you can add depth and richness to those populating your stories.

What is my character's name? Sometimes this will just be something that sounds right to you, sometimes there will be a deeper significance either to you personally, or to the plot in general, but in almost all cases, characters should have some form of name. (See the article on naming characters for a more in depth discussion about this.)

What does my character look like? Go all out on this. You might not use all the details but even if it only serves to set the character in your own mind so they are more real to you as you are writing, it strengthens your story and ultimately translates to the character being more real to the reader in the end. Also, there will be times when you need to distinguish between characters when their name doesn't come into play.

What is my character's personal background? I'm not just talking about what they do now, but where they came from, and who they hang out with, as well. Give at the very least your primary characters a history and some depth to their immediate lives. This includes family history, education, and even those deep, dark secrets we all have that we would rather no one else knew about. I'm not saying to weigh down your story with all of this stuff, but you don't know what will be relevant to the story until you are done. Do some preparation, have the information to hand, and that way as you are writing you can seed the story with whatever details flow in naturally. Even if something doesn't make it to the page it will still help you set in your own mind the appropriate reactions and personality traits of your character. By knowing where they've been you have a better understanding of who they are now.

What flaw does my character need to overcome? We all have them. There are always ways we can or outright need to improve. Don't neglect this aspect of your characters otherwise they will not only be flat and uninteresting, but also implausible. No one is perfect. Not even the make-believe. More than that, though, in fiction the flaws exist also to build tension, making them a vital tool.

Summing Up

Personality is important, as are physical traits. Not only do they give a sense of identity, but they also dictate what we — and our characters — are capable of. It is important for the author to have a firm grasp of that, particularly with longer works because if the details aren't locked down it is much easier for them to get jumbled as you go.

So You Think You Know...

(Originally published as Kelly Green, Corned Beef and Cabbage, and Other Stereotypes That Have Little or Nothing to Do With the Irish in the column If We'd Words Enough and Time)

Local color is very important in a story, it lends authenticity and helps draw the reader into whatever realm you want to immerse them.

It is so easy when writing to fall back on stereotypes that we have come to confuse with fact. In my early novels, *Yesterday's Dreams* and *Tomorrow's Memories*, I wrote about the Irish. Yeah, there is a wealth of stereotype there; some of it rooted in truth, and some of it made up either completely out of whole-cloth or based on outdated concepts more aptly termed — at least by me — Irish-Americanisms. Let's look at some of the misconceptions:

All Irish drink alcohol
If you are Irish you wear Kelly green
All Irish are religious
Corned beef and cabbage is an Irish dish

I am sure there are many more that we could come up with, but these are the most common, as well as the ones I discovered were not necessarily true when I actually went to Ireland. (Now, I focus on Ireland here only because it pertains to what I have written, but this applies to any culture or time period that you might have cause to write about.)

I know that stereotypes are a convenient and effective way to distinguish the locale or certain characters in a story, and if they are a minor part of the whole you may decide that for your purposes that is sufficient, however, when the element is a more significant part of your plot you want to depend on more than stereotype or your work will suffer.

If the place you want to capture in words is nearby then you are lucky. Just schedule a vacation or weekend get-away in your target area and talk to some people, see some sights, and sample the local flavor first hand. Now, if you are working with a culture that lies across an ocean you might not be able to indulge in a trip there to see for yourself the true local color that you want to capture in your writing. I didn't make it to Ireland until after my books were written, but a good Irish Pub helps fill in some of the details, (an authentic one, not just one capitalizing on the stereotypes, anyway.) This isn't always an option, though. There are several ways around not being able to visit the culture you want to write about:

- Internet sites dedicated to the region/culture you want to utilize
- Interviews with people originally from that area
- Visiting the cultural/ethnic neighborhoods found in many larger cities
- Research through books and local newspapers
- Phone calls to the Tourist Board for that area
- Slang dictionaries (regional and found on the internet)

Another facet of this dilemma is trying to write about a particular locale, but in a different time. Granted, unless there are people still living that may remember the time you are aiming at, then you are out of luck as far as interviews go—anyone have an extra time machine laying around anywhere?—but that doesn't mean that there isn't a wealth of information out there just waiting for you to dig in.

So You Think You Know... 39

Here are just a few sources you could plunder, and I am sure you can come up with a few on your own:

- Recreationalist groups (they exist for nearly every period in recorded history and for many cultures. The Society for Creative Anachronisms, or SCA, alone covers much more than just medieval England, for example.)
- Literary and journalistic archives (many libraries and universities have these going way back, and what you don't have in your local library you can often get through interlibrary loan. Microfilm is a bit trickier, but even that is migrating to the internet in many cases.)
- Old journals and letters (check with historic societies in the area you are focusing on)
- Museums and Historical Societies

These are by no means the only sources, just the first that come to mind. As writers there are many resources out there geared toward helping us get past the stumbling block of being born in a different era than that which we may want our stories to take place. For instance, the Writer's Digest Book Club alone has countless period reference books, such as *Everyday Life in the 1800's* and so on, not to mention guide books on making characters in different professions well... professional.

However you go about getting your information, remember this, your writing is only as good as the effort you put into it. If you want your work to be taken seriously, take a little time to do the research, make sure that your portrayals are more than just hasty stereotypes and flat depictions. The reader wants to see a world that comes alive through your words, not a two-dimensional view that merely mimics the world's preconceived notions.

Stereotypes might have their place, but it is not center stage and in the spotlight. Take the time to discover who your characters are and the worlds they really live in. Do justice to your work and to your readers. With so much research potential out there, particularly given the profusion of internet and TV documentaries geared toward just this sort of thing, building an accurate picture of something you have no exposure to at all on a regular basis is no longer the time-consuming excavation it once was.

Take a little effort... invest some time, you will be amazed at the difference it can make in your work.

The Tricky Art of Conversation

(Originally published in Allegory Magazine, www.allegoryezine.com)

There is no path so fraught with potential misstep than conversation. Bad enough talking to yourself — a whole other realm of fraught there — but bring another person into it and you get three things: What you said, what you thought you said, and what the other person heard.

Knowing what to say and when to say it… not so easy. *Am I getting my point across? Am I saying too much? Is this going to be taken wrong?* At some point we have all asked ourselves these questions; and that is just with verbal communication. Written dialogue… much more complex. And yet in fiction, as in life, conversations are what take you out of yourself — or the character's head — and integrate you into a living, breathing world.

Having trouble with that? Well, let's see if we can't extract your proverbial foot from your literary mouth…

What to Say

In writing, dialogue is one of the trickiest simple things to do. I know, contradiction, right? Not really. We talk every day. We hear people talk every day. It should be beyond easy to write two or more people holding a conversation.

Again, not really.

There are nuances of verbal communication that defy written expression, or at least are difficult to do full justice to. Expression, inflection, body language. Yes, you can include some or even all of that, but at what point does it begin to intrude, becoming cumbersome to read? Your task as a writer is to put in just enough cues to get your point across without slowing down the pace and flow inherent in natural conversation.

There are two ways you can learn this (besides through nifty how-to articles like this, which can only take you so far). First, go out and listen. Find a park or shopping mall or someplace where there are loads of people and sit yourself down. People watch, but more important, listen. Conversations are organic, each one unique. Some people are good at it and others aren't. By listening and observing you can get an objective feel for how different conversations proceed and what nonverbal vocabulary is involved.

Your second resource, read!

No, not a how-to book—I know, how ironic. One of the best ways to get the hang of written dialogue, or any other aspect of fiction writing, is to study what others have done... and sold! You want published examples for comparison because they have, in theory, been through the editing process. Now this doesn't guarantee they are examples of literary perfection but the works in print are representative of what is being accepted and published in today's market. You want to read more than a few books to get a proper feel for the dialogue. Pay attention not only to what is said and how, but to your own reaction to the author's attempt at replicating natural conversation. You don't necessarily need to read the full book—at least for the purpose of this exercise—skimming the dialogue should be enough to give you perspective (this might be a good time to dust off your library card). To save yourself some time, you might also ask your friends if they can recommend any books that had particularly good or bad dialogue.

Once you have a few examples of each, find a quiet place and try reading some of the selections out loud. This will help you identify the strengths and weaknesses in the written conversation. If something is awkward to speak aloud, it is usually awkward to read on the page as well, though that isn't always as consciously evident if you haven't first recited it. You might think if it isn't obvious, then it can't really be a problem, right? I wish, but the truth is that readers often pick up on these things on a subconscious level even if they can't readily identify why a particular passage is less effective or enjoyable than another.

Things you want to look for are comfortable pacing, dynamic exchange (meaning the back and forth between characters, not the snappy comebacks), conversational language suited to the character speaking, and nonverbal cues and clues. Everyone is going to have their own style, but dialogue should read like people actually speak, with appropriate tone for whatever setting it is occurring in.

The Art of It

Once you can recognize the mechanics of good dialogue it is time to move on to the conventions of conversation, more to the point, some of what to avoid.

Pace and Interaction. Think of dialogue as a tennis game. It's an exchange between two characters, sometimes recreational, sometimes competitive, occasionally adversarial, but always back and forth, like the ball going over the net. Think back on some of the conversations you've had in your life. I am sure there are those that ate away the hours without you realizing it because you were enjoying the exchange so thoroughly. By the same token, there were those you thought would never end. As an author, your objective is to find the right balance for the scene you are writing and the dynamics between the characters participating. Don't have one character dominate—unless, of course, that is the point—get a volley going. If one character goes on and on for some reason, make sure to interject with nonverbal reactions and exposition from the other character.

Information overload. Have you ever been trained in a job where the person training you just goes on and on, feeding you details without allowing you the chance to ask questions? If not, man, are you lucky! I can tell you that eventually, no matter how much you attempt to pay attention, your mind begins to shut off. There is only so much you can take in when you have no opportunity to process it. The same can happen in dialogue. If you have a character feeding detail after detail with very little interaction from the other character/s in the scene, the reader is going to miss some of what you wanted to get across. To avoid this, share the informational responsibility among your characters. Dialogue should be reactive: one character says one thing and the other has some kind of response, either through dialogue, nonverbal cues, or inner monologue. Dialogue should also be interspersed with action, otherwise the mind wanders. Come on, you know I'm right... just think about those family gatherings when you were young, expected to just sit there quietly as the adults talked around you. It is amazing the places the mind will take you faced with such tedium. Now, you don't want that for your readers, right?

Stating the obvious. There is no getting around the fact that everything you write on the page is meant to convey information to the reader. All of it. That's the entire point! One of the things you have to avoid, though, is being obvious about it. You want the reader to lose themselves in your universe, to be fully immersed in the story. The quickest way to yank them out of that immersion is to stage your dialogue in such a way that it is obviously there for the sole purpose of educating the reader. What do I mean by that? In a conversation with someone of a similar upbringing or whom you have an existing relationship with certain knowledge is common knowledge... to everyone but the newly introduced reader. One of the ways authors betray themselves is by have characters sharing information among themselves that they logically would have already been familiar with. It's kind of like when you want to tell someone something, but you don't feel you can directly, and instead you stage a conversation with someone else in front of that person so they overhear what you want them to know. Such conversations are rarely natural; same goes for dialogue.

Talking out of Character. If you have done your job properly each of your characters is going to some degree or other have a distinct personality. They will also have an established social position. This translates into a character's Voice (I'll be going into this in more depth in the next article: *Continuing the Conversation*). When writing dialogue, or even narrative, it is very important that your word choices for a character are in keeping with that Voice, otherwise you shatter the illusion you have built and the reader no longer believes in them.

Summing Up

Needless to say there is much more to dialogue than the little bit I've covered here. For now, follow the good examples, not the bad; remember to keep the right Voice in your head when writing from a particular character's point of view, and don't be a bore! Or rather, don't let your character's be, unless, of course that is their purpose in the tale.

Continuing the Conversation

(Originally published in Allegory Magazine, www.allegoryezine.com)

Do your characters talk to you? Come on, you can admit it.

No, really, it's a good thing!

Mine do—well, actually, they're more likely to argue with me, but that's beside the point…

If you can hear your characters in your head, clear and distinct and individual, that means they have their own Voice. Yes, Voice with a capital V. This is a very important part of the character's personality. With a capital V-Voice they have their own identity that sets them off from the other characters populating the story. Not just because you've said so, or because you've described them in very particular terms, or because of the things they say, but because the way they say them is unique only to them. Primarily, this pertains to dialogue, though not always. It depends on how much you use the narrative and point of view to establish your characters. For the purpose of this article we will focus on dialogue.

Getting the Conversation Started

So much of conversation is in how you say things. Your grasp of grammar—whether written or spoken—will determine how well you are understood. In person, you have the opportunity to clarify. On paper, you only get one chance. Because of this, even when you are trying to establish a character type you have to be sure to get your point across properly through word choice, sentence structure, and through the response of other characters, otherwise you are going to frustrate your reader. In my previous article, *The Tricky Art of Conversation*, I recommend reading selections of published dialogue to get a feel for what works and what doesn't. I again recommend that. My skill at writing effective dialogue without a doubt came out of my being a voracious reader since I was a young child. By the time I had to learn this stuff in school it was already coming naturally to me.

One of the most important things to remember is to break up your dialogue. Lectures, not conversations, are one person going on and on. Give your characters the opportunity to respond to one another, and if that isn't appropriate to the scene, inject a bit of narrative so we can see the silent participant's reactions to what is being said. In either case, always remember that more than one character is involved and don't let your reader forget either.

Personal Identity

Have you noticed in life how much you can tell about some people just from hearing them talk? I'm not talking friends, or family, or anyone you know intimately enough to pick up on the unspoken cues. I'm talking strangers, people you have just met. Now, as with most things in life, this doesn't go for everyone but there are several bits of personal information you can garner from a person's Voice — real life here, not fiction — those things are their general age, their gender, their education level, and their general geographic origins. This is because there are cues we all project without even realizing it. The words we choose, our diction, regional slang, or even just accent. These details are a part of our personal identity.

As writers it is our task to mimic those auditory cues to shape our characters. Now we are hindered a bit in this being a print medium — duh! — but by an intricate dance of narrative, dialogue, and character interaction you can accomplish the same goals. Let's look at the tools for the job:

Slang. This develops on several levels, for several reasons. Sometimes it comes out of technical language used among a given set of people, sometimes it is specific-use language developed by a ethnic or social group, or sometimes it stems from popular culture or results from poor education. Whatever the origin you need to take several things into account: the meaning of the slang, the context, and the appropriateness of its use by a particular character in a given situation. From my own works my novel, *The Halfling's Court*, is a perfect example. This book is set in my biker faerie universe — yes... I said *biker* faeries — and to write realistically in this context I had to do a lot of research into biker slang. I discovered they virtually have their own language, for instance, a mechanic is called a "Wrench," cars and their drivers are called "cages" and "cagers," respectively, and those thick, slick squiggles of tar used to repair cracks in the road are called "tar snakes," just to give you a sampling of what I mean.

Now, if we were to use this language in our everyday lives we would likely get more than a few eyebrows quirked at us, but in a biker bar, spoken with confidence and understanding, no one would bat an eye. I did not take myself down to the local biker bar, but I was very fortunate that there are a lot of websites on the internet that give a glossary of biker terms. Not only do they give you the language and the meaning, but they often put it in context as well. This made my job very simple and lent credibility to my biker characters. All it took was a little research. Of course, if you are lacking a convenient and detailed website, you can always interview someone of the appropriate demographic that uses the type of slang suited to the character you are trying to develop, or you can go to where such people are likely to be found and observe. Ironically enough, I've encountered this with the next installment of my biker faeries; that one includes roller derby girls and while I couldn't find a glossary on line, I was fortunate enough to contact the South Jersey Derby Girls and gained an invitation to one of their practices. We'll see how that one turns out. In the end, though, do the research, rather than relying on stereotypes and assumptions that may not be as authentic as you think they are.

Another caution, do not overdo this as it can become difficult for the reader if a story is too overloaded with such references, particularly if they are not intuitive to someone not a part of that culture. I always put a glossary in the back of my novels when I use a lot of slang or mythological references, but you also don't want to put your reader in the position of having to continually flip to the back just to understand what they are reading. Make your references clear and where necessary explain briefly and in a non-disruptive way in the context of the story.

Vocabulary/Grammar. This is related to slang, but not exactly the same. More often than not this is dictated by education level and career, though not always. Someone that is more well-read or educated might chose more complex words, or someone with a very technical occupation will reflect that in their speech. Of course, a character that wants to be perceived as well-read or educated might well adopt this manner of speech to mislead others.

Dialect. For our purposes, this is the written representation of regional accents. By itself it is only part of the picture but combined with the above two treatments it makes for a more three-dimensional character. Put into practice in literature it is generally the phonetic representation of some words or sounds representative of the verbal identity of an ethnic or regional group.

There are two schools of thought on this device. Some people absolutely loath written dialect. Others feel it has a transformative effect on the writing. In the end it all comes down to how you incorporate it. Done incorrectly — or correctly to excess — it can be tedious, even painful to read, especially if the character it is applied to is a primary focus character that appears and speaks often. With a lighter touch, it can be just enough to add flavor to a piece. But how do you decide how much is too much?

This is a dilemma I have run into personally. In my first novel, *Yesterday's Dreams*, three of my primary characters are Irish, complete with accent, as well as a number of secondary characters. It wasn't too bad, though I did catch some flack from reviewers. My approach to it was to take three conventions stereotypical of a brogue and apply them to those characters: the dropped consonant, primarily the "f" in of and the "g" in anything ending in –ing, substituting "ye" for "you," and " 'tis" and " 'twas" contractions. By selecting just these three alternations it was enough to get the point across without rendering the dialogue nearly indecipherable, as well as being easier to maintain consistency.

Pausing for a Breath

Now like I've said before, nothing is fool-proof or absolute. Take the above and consider it, then see how best to apply it to each character you write and specific interactions between those characters. If you are trying to set a particular feel, perhaps you want to go with a bit of dialect. If you need to establish a passing character quickly because they won't be around long, you might want to go with slang or specific vocabulary to get their Voice across. Whatever you chose, be consistent and don't let the device you use take undue attention away from the story you are telling. These are tools that should augment and complement your tale, not dominate them.

Wrapping Up the Conversation

(Originally published in Allegory Magazine, www.allegoryezine.com)

Dialogue is one of the writer's primary tools in mimicking real life. It can also be one of their greatest weaknesses. Good dialogue will do more to establish the personality of a character than any amount of description or narrative because, done correctly, it echoes things we have all experienced. Far-fetched as it might sound, you want the reader to forget they are reading… you want them to forget this is fiction. When your characters speak naturally through your words that state of immersion is possible. To accomplish this there are several things you need to understand about dialogue.

Identifying the Speaker

When you're having a conversation with someone, for the most part you know who is talking even when you can't see them. We have voice cues and context that help us distinguish the participants. In fiction, clearly, that aspect is missing. Instead the author must make plain which character is talking at any given time. There are several different schools of thought on this.

Stick with "said". When identifying the speaker some feel that substituting other words for "said" should be kept to a minimum. These individuals believe that "said" is one of those invisible words we are so used to that our eyes just gloss over it, acknowledging without catching on it or being disturbed by its repetition.

To substitute alternative words is to draw attention to the substitution and distract from the dialogue. For example:

>"I don't know what you mean," Corey said. "I have never been to that part of town."
>"But I was there, I saw you," Ralf said.

For the most part in literature, this is observed, particularly in traditional markets.

Vary your speech tags. Other people feel that the repetitiveness of "he said-she said" fosters an uncomfortable and obvious rhythm, particularly in dialogue-heavy passages. These individuals endorse using alternative words to "said" such as "commented," "answered," etc. Such substitution cuts down on the repetition, but can be more overt than simply saying said. For example:

>"When do you think you saw me there?" Corey asked.
>"Tuesday," Ralf responded.

(Personally, I prefer a happy medium between options one and two. If said suits, I use it, but if something else feels right, I substitute.)

Leave off the tag. No, not all together, all the time. But in a situation where the characters are established and it is clear who is talking, then yes, to improve the pace and flow of the dialogue, it is completely acceptable to have some of your dialogue go without a tag. For example:

>"Impossible!"
>"Well then you have a twin..." Ralf said, glaring at Corey. "And he's wearing the shirt I gave you for Christmas last year!"

Or

>"Impossible!"
>"That's interesting, Corey," Ralf said, "because you

were wearing the sweater you borrowed from me… the one my mom made for me!"

Alternate means of identifying the speaker. In some instances it is quite natural to use narrative or action to identify the speaker in place of the tag. For example:

> Corey whirled around. "I don't know what you mean. I have never been to that part of town."
> "But I was there, I saw you," Ralf said.

As you can see, there are many different options. The important thing is to pick the one that is comfortable for you, but also to be aware that when you are sending your work to a paying market, they might have their own preferences. See if the publication or publisher has a style guide on their website or if they mention a particular style guide they use, such as Chicago Manual of Style.

On a related note to the above, whether or not you use "said" or "commented" or some other alternative, keep in mind that word order is important, if it sounds awkward to read out loud then you shouldn't be using it in writing either. Word order is important and there is a current trend of writers transposing the subject and the verb in speech tags. For example:

> "But I was there, I saw you," said Ralf.

Now it might not seem like a big thing and when paired with a name it hardly seems wrong at all, but substitute a pronoun and the error glares:

> "But I was there, I saw you," said he.

Or substitute a different verb for just for the sake of example:

> "Ran he." versus "He ran."

Transposing a phrase might sound more poetic, or intimate, but many editors feel it is an indication of poor writing. So remember… noun first, then verb!

What to Talk About

Writers are faced with a particular challenge: how to convey necessary information to the reader without 1) resorting to info dumps, or 2) clearly leading the reader. The first is a conversation for another time. The second, though, applies to dialogue.

It is tempting to get your characters to do your dirty work for you, and don't get me wrong, that isn't a bad thing, you just have to be smart how you go about it. Unless you are writing for children give your reader credit for being observant. What do I mean by this? Don't spoon feed them, or write down to them. Written conversations between characters should be natural and purposeful. If you wouldn't have such a conversation in real life (personal circumstances aside) then your characters shouldn't be having it either. I'm not talking about the topics of conversation precisely, but the manner in which you conduct the conversation. Primarily, don't have your character regurgitate facts both of them clearly already know, when you do this you make it obvious that the conversation is being held for the purpose of the reader, rather than to advance the plot. If you want to reveal information by means of dialogue between characters be sure to weave in narrative to fill in those gaps in the reader's knowledge. For example:

> "I saw your sister, Tammy, the other day," Carl said, pausing as if not sure he should go on. "She looked good. Barely even limped."
>
> Ralf flinched. He hadn't seen her in months. Went out of his way to ensure he didn't. He was glad she was recovering from the accident but he didn't think he could face her yet. "Good. Good, I'm glad to hear it."

Now, you could argue that perhaps Ralf has more than one sister, in which case it would be natural for Carl to specify which one. On the other hand, I could argue that the name would be sufficient because after all, Ralf will know who Tammy is by context if nothing else, but as an example, let's assume there is both one sister and one Tammy. Here's how I would fix this:

"I saw your sister the other day," Carl said, pausing as if not sure he should go on. "She looked good. Barely even limped."

Ralf flinched. Tammy. He hadn't seen her in months. Went out of his way to ensure he didn't. He was glad she was recovering from the accident but he didn't think he could face her yet. "Good. Good, I'm glad to hear it."

Or

"I saw Tammy the other day," Carl said, pausing as if not sure he should go on. "She looked good. Barely even limped."

Ralf flinched. He hadn't seen his sister in months. Went out of his way to ensure he didn't. He was glad she was recovering from the accident but he didn't think he could face her yet. "Good. Good, I'm glad to hear it."

Establishing Personality

You have surely noticed that what a person says isn't always as important as the way they say it, right? This is applicable for personality, as well as intent.

"I don't know what you mean," Corey said, with a sly glint in his eye. "I have never been to that part of town."

Or

"I don't know what you mean," Corey said, his expression baffled. "I have never been to that part of town."

Or

"Dude, I don't know what you're talking about," Corey said, his expression sullen and his posture slouched.

Both word choice and physical description in the speech tags can in a few short words define a character, either overall or in reaction to a given situation.

The Final Word

So, when you sit down to write—dialogue or narrative—remember what your purpose is: to establish your characters and universe in a non-obtrusive manner, allowing the reader to immerse themselves in the reality you have built as completely as they are able, without the presence of the author intruding overtly on the experience. To accomplish this through dialogue, ask yourself the following questions:

- Is this a natural conversation?
- Does it convey knowledge already common to the character?
- Would this be better expressed in narrative?
- Does the dialogue fit the personality I have established for the character in question?
- What does the dialogue do to advance the plot or inform the reader of the back story?

Be natural, be age-appropriate (to your readers and your characters!), think of the words as actually coming out of a person's mouth. Better yet, get someone to read through it with you, each of you taking an appropriate character's lines of dialogue. See if your dialogue holds up as a conversation. Artificial dialogue can be the kiss of death to a good story. I know I myself see it almost as a personal affront when characters come across as patently fake independent of anything required by the plot. Look closely at your characters, be true to them and let *them* talk.

Spend Your Words Wisely

(Originally published in the column If We'd Words Enough and Time)

How many words does it take to tell a story?

Can't really answer that, can we? Or at least, not easily... There are too many variables, too many considerations. Is it a short story? A long one? A novel? A complex, or a simple one? What do you want to tell? What do you want to simply imply?

Who can say, really? A haiku can convey a story in seventeen syllables; Tolstoy required thousands of pages. Most of us are fortunate, we can answer the original question as simply as this: It takes as many words as it takes.

But then, who wants to be simple, anyway? In this world of done and redone and overdone, we want a challenge, don't we? At the time this article was originally written such websites as New Times – San Luis Obispo and AOL's Amazing Instant Novelist — and who knows how many others over the years — offered up that challenge every day: write a complete and compelling story in however many words strikes the sponsor site's fancy and no more. Usually they are generous, allowing a few hundred, at least. A challenge, but a relatively simple one.

Not so with New Times – San Luis Obispo. Are you ready for this? Maybe you better sit down... fifty-five words a story, nothing more!

Can't be done, you say? Well, there's the challenge, and the guidelines are very specific as to what constitutes a story: one or more characters, a setting, a conflict, and a resolution. It ain't easy (ooh! I can hear my grade school English teacher screeching from her grave, now!), but it can be done, as I will show you below. With the permission of my illustrious... anonymous partner in crime — let's just call him IrateIndigoSimian, why don't we? — I'd like to give you an example of the same story from a couple of different approaches:

> He had always loved her, ever since the first time he had laid eyes on her he had known she was the only one. He kissed her sleeping forehead gently and considered her betrayal.
> The recoil from the gun surprised him, the finality of it all didn't. He turned the gun toward himself next.

Simple... straightforward... uncomplicated. Nothing wrong with that. By the contest guidelines, this definitely works, but does it work well? Think about it, the author made use of all of his fifty-five words, "had" was used three times, "her" was used four times, and "he" was used five times; those three words make up more than twenty percent of the author's allotment. Ouch! Yeah, it works, but the impact the subject matter could have is diminished by the frivolous use of throw-away words. (Don't feel I'm being too harsh with IrateIndigoSimian, this was a first draft. We already hashed all of this out and he agrees.) Now, let's look at a later version of the story:

> Their love had been the thing keeping him alive for years now. Her betrayal severed their bond, his soul, his mind. His final kiss left a soft, warm ghost touch on her sleeping forehead.
> The recoil from the gun surprised him, the finality of it all didn't. He turned the gun toward himself next.

Not bad, this version has a decidedly different feel, putting everything out in the reader's face from the very beginning. You are immediately confronted with the character's betrayal and anger, and the ending is a logical progression, without surprise. This accomplishes something very different from the first draft, and as for economy, not one word, other than articles, appears more than three times. This is an honest, straightforward rendition of this piece, but for my own tastes, a little too much in your face, not subtle enough.

Now for a bit more subtlety: The next one is more ambiguous. Other than the main character's love, we aren't sure how this is going until the fourth line. With the emotions drawn on, the fondness that is admitted, the second paragraph is a shocker:

> He found he couldn't remember a time he hadn't loved her. Even now, his soul was entwined with hers. Her sleep was deceptively peaceful. He gently kissed her cool forehead and contemplated her betrayal.
>
> The recoil from the gun surprised him, the finality of it all didn't. He turned the gun toward himself next.

And the last is on a similar vein, with the betrayal hinted at in the third line, but not revealed until the fourth. This draws the reader in, hooks them, has them guessing. The words chosen have an emotional impact all their own; you feel his love, then his betrayal… and finally, your own shock:

> There was never a time he hadn't loved her. Even now, his soul was entwined with hers. She slept so sweetly… innocently… deceptively so. He gently kissed her cool forehead and contemplated her betrayal.
>
> The recoil from the gun surprised him, the finality of it all didn't. He turned the gun toward himself next.

With all fiction, and most decidedly in microfiction—or drabbles, as they are now called—you have to choose carefully. Think of the emotional investment of the words you put to the page… for example, in the last line of the first paragraph, the first version has the main character "considered" the woman's betrayal, in subsequent versions it was changed to "contemplated"… Considered is an everyday word, an ordinary word. Contemplated is more involved, more impact.

It is cliché, but no matter what the length of your prospective work you need to go for quality, not quantity, but most especially with something like this, where you only have so many words to use... each one has to score.

Words should have purpose, a goal, all of them used to good effect. Unless it is for a reason, never use more words than you have to; your work can drown in a profusion of "highfalutin' " words, as my Daddy liked to tell me. Use a fancy word because it lends something, because it enriches the beauty of your poetry or prose; by the same token, do not be afraid to use a simple "workaday" word, if it suits your purposes. Simply put, use a word because it does what you need it to do, not because it is delightfully pretentious.

And finally, because it bears repeating over and over — ironically enough — when you are writing and rewriting your work, no matter the length, always keep close watch, guarding against our natural impulses to repeatedly use the same familiar words, even if we have used them three times already on the same page. Many word processors (if not *all*) have a Thesaurus option, my greatest advice to you: use it.

Literary Detailing

You know, sometimes we just don't know when to stop. No. It's true, even I'm guilty (I know. *Shocker*.) We get so caught up in the language and discovery of these worlds in our head that we just pile on the detail. We get so caught up in the creativity that we have to build the universe right down to the thumbtacks on the wall, or we're worried about not being clear, or missing something important, until we end up with a literal checklist of all the steps that took our characters from A to B… for each scene.

Okay, so perhaps I exaggerate, but not completely. There are times in fiction that call for expansive detail and others where too much clutter kills the action. It is important to know how and when to hold back. There are two kinds of detail: relevant information, and window dressing. The relevant details might be regarding the character, the setting, or the plot; the stuff you must tell the reader for the story to work. The window dressing is what helps your story really come alive. It is what the characters experience through their five senses, the type of detail you would casually take note of in your day-to-day life.

Now, if you do your job properly, every part of your story will combine the above types of details with only the degree of each varying, but each scene will have a central focus: Some scenes are so you can get to know the characters and their conflicts and drives, some reveal details you'll need to know to understand what is going on, and others propel the story forward. What type of scene you are writing will determine how much detail is called for, and what type.

Plot-oriented scenes. These scenes are what we call the build-up. Something happens, or someone says something, or the protagonist finds — sometimes knowingly, but often not — the key to resolving everything. The reader learns where things are, how they work, and what's important. There is going to be detail there. Some of it is the whole point of the scene and sprinkled around that detail is backdrop, either to mask that this is an important detail or just to flesh out the scene so that it is not static.

Character-oriented scenes. For these scenes everything should be in terms of how it relates to the character: their motivations, their past, their goals. And let's not forget, their features and personality. Readers need to get to know your characters so depending on their level of importance, some characters get a little detail, some a lot. Inner monologues and self-examination are not frowned upon here, unless they go on for too long, but they shouldn't dominate the storyline. Of course, that also depends on the type of characters in the scene. Protagonists we should know like our own blood because we need to care what happens to them. Secondary characters, we should know their importance to the protagonist and some small amount of detail that impacts the story or their actions. Background characters, something to identify them, a name or a feature, but nothing else that doesn't directly relate to the scene they appear in or the part they play in the plot.

Action-oriented scenes. In most action scenes you either already know all or most of the players, or they are only relevant for what they are doing at the moment. This is about what is happening, what blows are struck and what plans are put into action… reactions and movement. The setting is only important in relation to its impact on the characters and its impact on what is taking place. You want short, sharp sentences where things are happening, not exposition or distraction.

Things to Consider

Once you have a handle on what scenes you are writing, here are some questions to help you keep focused as you tackle each one:

Is the scene a destination or a transition? If it is the former you have more leeway to go into detail because that is the point. If a scene is a transition you want to focus more on relevant details, rather than background stuff. Now, there is a caveat: if the point is to show an extended passage of time, expounding a bit more is to be expected.

Is it taking too long to get where you're going? If you personally start to feel like things are dragging, then that is a sure sign that they are. Pacing is important and too much detail can slow things down. Go back over the story and pare things back. Shorten sentences, take out detail you don't really need, even cut out whole sections and give us a fade-away before cutting to another character or just a later point in the story.

Is the detail relevant later? Sometimes we just put in detail because it is cool, and sometimes we mention something that seems totally irrelevant, but the entire story hinges on it. Be careful of focusing on something that isn't a key point too heavily because readers have come to assume that anything the author spends an extended time on will be important. It leaves them frustrated at the end if some such point turns out to be merely fluff.

Summing Up

Details are what will define your story: they are the building blocks of your universe, the soul of your characters. Be a little coy, be a little bold, and always proceed at the proper pace for the scene you are writing. Don't be afraid of detail or ignore it, but don't let it run away with you either.

Coming to Your Senses

No! Not like that. I know what it is like to have the writing bug. When you really have it, there's no getting rid of it. I'm talking the five senses, not common sense.

One thing I've learned over the years is that we pick up a lot of information in our day-to-day lives, most of it without even realizing. There is a constant influx of sights, sounds, smells, tastes, and touches. This influx helps us to define our world. Remove any one or more of these senses and the rest have to work that much harder.

Writers would do well to remember that. And I don't mean in relation to the characters.

I can see the look on your face now. *Huh?*

Let me explain. As writers one of our jobs is to create a world that the readers will be drawn into. For that to happen it has to be presented so that they can relate. We process our world through our senses. If you neglect that in your writing or depend only on the more common senses of sight, sound, and perhaps smell, those senses will have to work very hard to connect the reader with your created world, which will lack some of the dimension we've come to expect in life.

Now, I'm not saying to bombard the reader to the extent that a snail would move faster than your plot, but there are natural openings for sensory data in most fiction and those openings often go underutilized. You don't want paragraphs of nothing but description, but you can do a lot to integrate both your character and the reader into a setting by weaving in sensory data as the action progresses.

First, let's see what we have to work with:

Sight. Most authors have this one down pretty good. After all, we know you have to describe what's going on, and what is seen, right? In shorter works you mostly want to keep this down to relevant details, basic description of the setting or things that the characters are seeing as they move about. More focus is placed on something that is a key point in the story with the rest just setting the scene. In longer fiction, however, there is room to play.

Sound. The obvious things here are sudden sounds meant to indicate something is about to happen, or dialogue, but our world is so full of background sounds. That is where you will find depth in your literary universe. Children laughing. The sounds of cars. Birds singing. The argument down the street. These are common, every-day things. They are the pulse of life itself. Have your character note such sounds… or even the absence of such sounds, which can communicate a lot to the reader.

Smell. Again, often used in fiction to indicate something out of the ordinary; an alert that we should pay attention, but smells seem to be the sense most linked to memories. I know personally that the scent of the air just around mid-October, or early November has a distinct difference and I respond to that each time I smell it. Just mention that crisp, slightly mulchy aroma and all kinds of associations come to my mind: from raking multicolored leaves to the nip in the air on a Halloween night to the heavy weight of my cold-weather coat.

Taste. This doesn't just come into play when you eat or drink. Sometimes a scent on the air or clinging dust or any one of a myriad of things we encounter each day that touches or passes our lips. By choice or otherwise! Those things can tell you much about a setting or situation. Do not overlook this aspect of our environment. Sometimes we as writers even associate tastes with emotional responses, a good way to incorporate them when the actual taste buds are not possibly engaged.

Touch. There is no point in life when we are not touched by something: a breeze, a falling leaf, someone brushing by. When all of our other senses fail us, this is for the most part the one to remain faithful. In very few instances can we move about and not come in contact with our environment in some way. Our characters should likewise interact with their world.

A Matter of Depth

You knew all the above... pretty much, yes? It's a given. We don't think about it much, but there are certain things we just know. These are the simple basics of reality. Incontrovertible facts. When you are building a world, though, it is very important to go beyond the basics. Don't assume that the reader will get the depth of detail you are looking if you aren't giving them any cues. For example:

>Tammy's coat brushed against Kyle's hand.

That tells us what happened, but not really anything else. What you want are the tactile clues that will resonate with the reader. Yes, with the above they will likely have a memory or some idea of what the sensation is like just from their own experience, but what if their experience isn't what you are going for? For example, what if you had something like this in mind:

>Tammy brushed past Kyle, the heavy wool of her coat slapping hard against his hand.

>Or

>Kyle shivered at the slap of wet wool against his hand as Tammy brushed past him.

Both sentences basically say the same thing as far as the action goes, but the choice of adjectives gives very different sensory input. Don't leave all the work up to the reader; for your story to work you need to give the audience the proper cues. Okay. Let's take it a little further with the next example:

> The lights were off when Ricki arrived home. She unlocked the door and stepped inside. Moving carefully through the room she turned on the lights. Mac was sprawled on the floor.

You know the progression, but you don't know how Ricki feels and you don't get any sense of her interacting with her world. There is plenty of action/reaction, but as a reader you don't know how to react yourself to the words on the page. Now try this:

> The autumn breeze took on a deeper chill as Ricki pulled up in front of the house. The windows were dark and there were deep shadows around the door. The porch light was out, as was every light in the house. Ricki drew a sharp breath and scrambled out of the car as soon as it was in park. The door knob was icy beneath her hand as she unlocked the front door. Even before she stepped inside a metallic tang pinched her nose. A soft groan sounded from the darkness. With shaking hands she flipped on the light. Mac blinked up at her from where he sprawled on the floor, his expression dazed by more than just the sudden light.

This paragraph not only paints a picture for the reader, but gives cues on how the reader is supposed to feel. Yes it took longer, but this isn't a trip to the store we are talking about, it is an adventure in a brand new world.

Summing Up

It is a common adage in writing: Show, don't tell. The best way to do that is letting your character experience their reality through sensory input that will resonate with the reader. Think about what you want to convey not just about what your character is experiencing, but their surroundings and the emotional responses you want to inspire in any given scene. Every encounter will not call for all five senses, but engage them, when you can, more than singly or in pairs. After all, it is up to us as writers to create a comprehensive experience for the reader as they wander the pages of our universes.

The Short and the Long of a Novel Idea

I was recently approached by an aspiring novelist. This writer was stymied because he wanted to write a novel, but his stories kept wrapping up in about fifty pages or less (assuming standard margin and double spacing, probably about 20 to 30,000 words) which makes them technically novellas. This is a common dilemma for writers, wanting to write a novel, but not knowing how to get started.

Let's start by looking at the difference between a short story and a novel. (besides word count, smart aleck!)

Well, part of what makes a short story different from a novel is back story; most short fiction has just the relevant information to the story being told. Novels, on the other hand, explore characters and events a bit more, including information that is not necessary to the story, but does develop the character or give the reader insight to why things are the way they are. You can also explore the setting in a bit more detail and that kind of thing. All of this makes for a richer, more layered universe where the reader gets the feeling that there are other, unseen things going on in the world around the characters.

The second thing that is the major difference between short stories and novels is multiple threads. Usually there is one overall plot to a short story and that is it. Novels have a primary plot, but a number of subplots that are related in some way but still differ from the main goal of the story. Sometimes the subplot will deal with the main character and sometimes it will be a separate story line where another character is the focus and your main character is secondary. So basically think of a novel as telling several stories at once, but interwoven.

To use a metaphor... novels are woven tapestries, whereas short stories are knitted afghans. Many individual threads versus one continuous yarn (for simplicity's sake, though there are always exceptions).

Start out with your characters and figure out three things about each one:

- What is their goal?
- What do they have to do to achieve that goal?
- What is preventing them from achieving that goal?

Sometimes there will be multiple answers to each of the above, but don't make it too complicated... Also, don't be afraid to alter things as you go. I start out with an idea and write a bit, then do some research related to what I've written and often that sparks other ideas relevant to what I am doing but different from what I'd planned. My work has much more life in it if I let it develop organically rather than sticking rigidly to my plan. Other writers put together an outline that lays out the key points of the entire novel. Some write the way I write, no method is more correct than another, so find the way that works for you.

Another method I have used is to write a number of short stories in the same universe, with the same characters. This has the same basic effect as a novel, particularly if you have an overall theme that continues from story to story, with a secondary theme that resolves itself by the end of the individual story. Each story should stand alone so that if anyone reads just that one, they won't feel lost or that they are missing part of the picture. Once you are done you can go back and link them into one big storyline, revising to take out repetitive detail, or just leave the stories as is and publish it as a collection instead of a novel, but with the same effect.

I'll give you an example from my own experience:

My novel, *The Halfling's Court: A Bad-Ass Faerie Tale*; when I first introduced my biker faeries of the Wild Hunt M.C. in the anthology *Bad-Ass Faeries* it was meant to be a stand-alone story. Entitled "At the Crossroads," the story dealt with a faerie challenge, but set in the modern day. Since it was a short story I put more effort into setting the feel of the universe than going in-depth into the characters motivations. Those I kept simple. Faerie biker wants faerie woman, faerie woman goes missing, faerie biker must ride to the rescue. As I said, I never meant it to be anything more… however… the story was so well received that when we went back to do the second volume in the series, *Just Plain Bad*, I decided to write in the same universe, this time with a story called "Within the Guardian Bell," borrowing on both faerie lore and biker lore pertaining to road gremlins. Again, the story was well-received.

I should not have been surprised when shortly thereafter a publisher showed interest in a Wild Hunt novel.

This posed quite a challenge for me because as I mentioned, the stories were meant to just be stories, and now I had to incorporate them into a novel. The character development was not as detailed as I would have done for a novel, but by the same token the writing was tightly woven, making it difficult to interject new copy building on the characters more. I managed, but not to everyone's satisfaction. From this I have learned that when I am writing a short story I will take the extra space and flesh out the characters a little more than necessary.

In addition to adding character detail and integrating new characters, I had the challenge of pruning away redundant details. After all, the stories originally were linked, but printed separately so enough detail had to be recapped from one to the other so that no matter which story was read, the person reading it didn't feel lost. This had the added benefit of tightening the writing and smoothing out the pace. When gathering related stories into a collection this is not so much of a concern as it is when you are fully integrating them into a novel, but still be aware of details too often repeated and perhaps edit them out in a few instances.

Now, when I was writing *The Halfling's Court* I was aware a third *Bad-Ass Faeries* anthology was coming up, so rather than have three stories all integrated into the same novel, I instead left a gap in the manuscript where some of the secondary action takes place off-page. I later came back and wrote that scene as a stand-alone story, "Seeing Red," which is also the linking story between *The Halfling's Court* and the upcoming sequel, *The Redcaps' Queen*.

So, as you can see, if you goal is a novel but it seems too daunting a task, try establishing a 'universe' through a series of short stories and you never know what might develop!

Writing Exercises

This section is meant to complement the articles you just completed reading. They are exercises I have used in writing seminars over the years and have found useful. I hope you do as well. There is one exercise to a page so that you may photocopy them if you wish to complete the exercise on the page with the instructions for reference. Feel free to do so for the purpose of honing your craft.

As mentioned in my opening note, there is no particular order here. Have fun!

Writing Exercise – Character Development: Take fifteen minutes and write a scene that starts off with the following elements (you can elect to add other elements and characters): A woman in one shoe, a broken branch, and a public place. Remember to show who your character is through action, thought, and expression. (Aim for 200 to 300 words).

Writing Exercise – Writing to the Senses: For each of the following listings write down three descriptions for each of the five senses (not all the senses will apply).

Example: A Fishing Wharf
Sight:
1. a long expanse of weathered pier,
2. sun sparkling off the water,
3. a lone pole propped against the rail

Smell:
1. the tang of brine on the wind,
2. the tarry aroma of the sun-heated planks,
3. the scent of roasting peanuts from a nearby vendor

Sound:
1. the strident cry of the gulls,
2. the gentle slap of water against the pilings,
3. the hissing zip of a cast fishing line

Taste:
1. a hint of salt as the surf sends a mist into my face,
2. the beefy taste of hot dog I bought on the boardwalk,
3. the flavor of fish

Touch:
1. the wet slap of a caught fish,
2. rough wood beneath my fingers,
3. the breeze tugging on my hair

A City Street Corner
Sight:
1.
2.
3.
Smell:
1.
2.
3.
Sound:
1.
2.
3.
Taste:
1.
2.
3.
Touch
1.
2.
3.

A Room in an Abandoned Building
Sight:
1.
2.
3.
Smell:
1.
2.
3.
Sound:
1.
2.
3.
Taste:
1.
2.
3.
Touch
1.
2.
3.

A Battlefield
Sight:
1.
2.
3.
Smell:
1.
2.
3.
Sound:
1.
2.
3.
Taste:
1.
2.
3.
Touch
1.
2.
3.

An Art Studio
Sight:
1.
2.
3.
Smell:
1.
2.
3.
Sound:
1.
2.
3.
Taste:
1.
2.
3.
Touch
1.
2.
3.

82 The Literary Handyman

Writing Exercise – Writing to the Senses, Part Two: Write a brief scene based on one of the settings in the previous exercise, incorporating the details you have listed (you do not have to use all of them, just what fits the scene).

Writing Exercise – Description: Take four canvas bags or something you cannot see through. Have someone place a different item in each bag where you cannot see what they have put inside. These should be things that have very distinct textural feels. Reach in to each one, do not look, and then describe the contents in the space below. The object is not to guess or tell what the items are, but to express the tactile nature of the item.

1)

2)

3)

4)

Writing Exercise – The Five Senses: Do this as a group exercise, if possible. Gather a notebook, pen, blindfold, earplugs, and something to plug your nose, then take a field trip to somewhere with a lot of sensory input (if you are self-conscious, you can do this without the last three items); try a mall, the beach, a park or something similar. Once you are there attempt to isolate your senses one at a time, or at the least, focus on them individually. (Taste will be the most difficult. Try breathing through your mouth to capture elements on the air, or having the group provide you with edible things from where you happen to be.) Take some time with this and try and pinpoint the various sensory data you gather, as many things as possible for each sense (not all will apply), then write them down in your notebook. As a group, compare the different information you gathered. Save the notes for future use in your fiction.

Writing Exercise – Character Development: Take fifteen minutes and write a brief description of the following characters. Give them a name, a history, and physical and personality traits, and one character strength and one character weakness. Describe only, this is not a story.

A young woman in her twenties.

A little boy, no younger than three, no older than twelve.

Writing Exercise – Dialogue: Write three lines of dialogue to suit the description given. Keep in mind the character should be identified first, then the attribution (She said; Kyle replied, not said she or replied Kyle). Or experiment with using action and reaction to identify the speaker, rather than "she said."

1) argumentative:
"Don't bother to lie to me!" she said, her teeth gritting. "I found the receipt from the motel in your pocket."

2) romantic:
Tammy looked up at him through lowered lashes, a half smile tugging at her lips. "I don't have anywhere I need to be... unless you have somewhere to suggest?"

3) frightened:
"I... it was right there, I swear it was," Kyle stammered, the whites fully visible around his irises.

4) hurt:
"You know," she said, her voice low and trembling, "I expected that kind of thing from her... but... but you?"

5) excited:
"We won! Oh my God! We won!" She grabbed her partner by the shoulders and danced around with glee.

Writing Exercise – Dialogue: Time for another field trip. Go to a populated location and observe a nearby conversation. You don't need to be close enough to hear. Take notes on the nonverbal cues in the conversation, expression, body movement, vocal tone (if you can hear it). Write your own dialogue to match the observed cues, incorporating them into the narrative.

Writing Exercise – Characterization: Complete this exercise with a fellow writer or in a group. Take a primary character you have already created and write down everything you know about them. Be as thorough as possible, including physical and personality traits as well as personal history. Give that character sheet to your partner (you should receive one in return) and then each of you write a scene or short story utilizing the description you were given. Do not add character details beyond those provided. When complete, exchange and read what the other person has done with your character, noting the differences from your own interpretation and looking for gaps in the profile that leave your character less defined than you may have realized.

Writing Exercise – Local Color: Take a social or ethnic group you are familiar with and write a scene depicting the distinctive elements of that group. Do not depend on cliché, but rather things you have observed or experienced first hand. This can also be done as a field trip, though you should use caution in selecting the environment you enter for this purpose.

Writing Exercise – Naming/Characterization: This is a good exercise to do in a group. Make three separate lists of names, (first, last, and nicknames.) Have fun with it. For best results, make sure the names reflect diversity. You should have an equal number of each, but they should be separate lists. Take scissors and cut those lists into little strips containing one name each, keeping the piles separate. Put the first, last, and nicknames in separate bowls. Pick one slip of paper from each bowl and write down the resulting name. Take a few moments and write a brief description of that character to match the name. Be sure to include ethnic background and an explanation of how the character acquired the nickname.

Business

Always Another Day Away

(Originally published in the column If We'd Words Enough and Time)

So... you wonder why you don't get any writing done... right? Let me guess... Work gets in the way? You have Writer's Block? You're tired? You're not good enough? *Enh*... Wrong answer.

Procrastination... The Lazy-Eyed Monster

First off, let's see what Merriam-Webster's Colligate Dictionary has to say on this subject:

> Main Entry: **pro·cras·ti·nate**
> Function: *verb*
> Inflected Form(s): **-nat·ed; -nat·ing**
> Etymology: Latin *procrastinatus*, past participle of *procrastinare*, from *pro-* forward + *crastinus* of tomorrow, from *cras* tomorrow
> Date: 1588
> *transitive senses* : to put off intentionally and habitually
> *intransitive senses* : to put off intentionally the doing of something that should be done
> **synonym** see DELAY
> - **pro·cras·ti·na·tion**
> - **pro·cras·ti·na·tor**

So, you might say: No way! I would never *intentionally* put off writing, so this doesn't apply to me. *Enh*... wrong again... All of us do it, from time to time, me most of all. When I originally wrote this it was 7:16pm on Saturday night... guess when this column was due? Yup, Saturday. We may not realize we are doing it, but we are constantly making decisions that stand in the way of our writing progress.

It Will Just Take a Few Minutes...

What is it for you? Do you have to clean up the mess before you can concentrate? Do you need to catch that season finale, or you just won't be able to think straight? How many times have you gone for a snack? Or decided to check your email first? There are so many little things that get in the way of what we "really" want to do: write. To be truthful, I am sure that you don't even realize you are doing it; I know I don't most the time. The truth is the few minutes those tasks take can really add up.

How do you get around this? Writing time is writing time, baring emergencies — or impending spousal wrath — nothing is to interrupt it. Don't have a TV nearby, make sure your family stays clear (with the noted exception of the above instances), make sure your hunger and thirst contingencies are in place, and close your mind to the world outside your writing space. (This is not recommended for long stretches of time, unless you want those close to you to forget what you look like).

To Muse or Be-Muse?

Acceptance is the first step. Now repeat after me: I am a procrastinator. Very good... Now, do you know why? Everyone has their own reasons — admittedly, sometimes even valid.

A lack of inspiration. It can be rough not knowing what to write. I have definitely been there myself, from time to time. The ways I get around this, editing and assignments. If I find myself with a lack of inspiration — the dreaded Writer's Block — I do not let it stand in my way. You may not make headway in your storyline, but if you at the very least use your writing session to review what you have already written it serves several purposes: one, it allows you to catch mistakes like spelling and grammar; two, it gives you an opportunity to flesh out any sections that need it; and three, it re-familiarizes you with the work you have already done. All three of these can help summarily banish your lack of inspiration.

Another way around this is to use an outline, or keep a list of "things I need to write." I don't work well with an outline because I'm always radically diverging from it, but I do create lists in relation to my novels. I jot down any ideas or elements I want to be sure to incorporate in the finished product. When I find myself stumped and I have already polished what I've written before to a fare-thee-well, I read through my notes and ideas. It doesn't always work, but nothing will, every time. If nothing else, it does remind me of my goals.

If you don't have an ongoing project to help you along, have someone provide you with assignments, topics or situations for you to base your work on as an exercise. Think about it… most of us fell in love with writing thanks to some English teacher somewhere. Assignments and reports fostered our interest and cultivated our enthusiasm (presuming you did well at them, but then, if you hadn't you likely wouldn't be reading this, would you?)

For most of us, that is the seed that got this obsession started. But seeds need to be tended or they shrivel and die. How many of you realized that after the impetus of school was removed from your daily routine, your writing efforts became drastically reduced? I know mine did. It wasn't the enjoyment that fled, just the motivation. There was no sense of direction anymore. So recreate it. I had a friend give me assignments and I also found an on-line writing site with weekly writing contests. Without that, I never would have been published when I was. Whatever means you use to get past this stumbling block, be sure to write. Some in the industry insist that you must write every day, or you aren't a writer. I'm more practical than that. Life does get in the way, after all. To me as long as you make the effort to write *something* on a relatively regular basis, then you're still in the game. It is vital to write, though; to let your creativity out to play. It is the only way for your talent to grow.

Why Do Today What You Can Put Off 'Til Tomorrow?

Too much effort. I don't know about you, but I am lazy to the extreme when it comes to certain aspects of my writing. Part of this stems from too many steps, part comes from too much waiting, and yet another part comes from too much doubt. See, in my own experience, to use a cliché we can all relate to, I am used to being a big fish in a little pond and a little fish in the big pond.

I don't find writing to be too much of a problem, most of the time. In fact, I have more problems stopping when I *should* be doing other things. My biggest problem, and the source of my private procrastination habits, is in submitting my finished work for consideration in the various venues that exist for authors. It isn't a lack of desire to gain recognition. It isn't a lack of confidence in my talent. It is an overwhelming aversion to waiting and wondering. This will explain to you how, though I have written prolifically since the age of thirteen, it wasn't until I was thirty-one that my work was recognized in any way.

This is the roadblock that I must work my way past. So far, even now, I have made little effort to submit my work to any venue unless it was the simplest of procedures, or I felt I had something to set me off from being just another faceless by-line. I like places that accept electronic submissions (they tend to respond quicker) and if I have an introduction to those reviewing submissions, or even better, a previous connection to them, that is when I submit. I still look for those places I can submit electronically because it cuts out the transit-time portion of the waiting, but I have worked my way from submitting only when my work is solicited, or submitting when my work is recommended. The next step I have taken is to aggressively seek out sources that don't know me from Eve. It is tough for me, learning to wait patiently to see if any will find a home, but it is the next step in my professional growth. I know my work is appreciated by those that are familiar with it... but those professionals that are seeing it for the first time... daunting.

Why? Because despite what I have accomplished in the last nine years, my reason for procrastinating is a fear of rejection… a fear that this isn't good enough…

I resolve that I will work my way past that fear.

Now, my friend, you need to look at your own personal brand of procrastination and see what is required of you to overcome it. Only by freeing our dreams can they be realized.

In Godhood Is Perfection Found

(Originally published in the column If We'd Words Enough and Time)

… And nowhere else. Remember that. It's important.

You've written the next Great American Novel… you bask in the glow of the accomplishment and look down on all non-achievers with faint (and certainly justifiable) condescension. Neatly typed in complete observance of the submission guidelines of all the major publishers, you are ready for your deserved acclaim.

Yeah… it was kind of hard for me to not let it go to my head too… until my first less-than-glowing review came through citing the fact that my precious masterpiece was riddled with flaws even a mediocre editor should have caught. I learned an important lesson that day, and once I started rewriting *Yesterday's Dreams,* I had to admit the reviewer in question, as well as the three or four others that shared his opinion, were completely right. My story was delightful; my grasp of certain aspects of grammar was not.

Now, no publisher expects a manuscript to be flawless… if they did, copyeditors across the country would have no jobs. The lesson I have learned from this experience… well… the three lessons I learned from this experience, in fact, are as follows:

- Always remember the adage "To Err is Human…"
- Never assume my work is pristine
- And, never assume the editor will catch all my mistakes

I know! I know! That is what editors are there for, right? Well, you know, that is logical in theory, but all too often books are launched onto the shelves with absolutely no consideration given to the errors within, either because the publisher wants to save the cost of paying a copy editor or because they are in a rush to get the book on the shelves and assume the corrections can be done later. Besides, even if the copyeditor *does* practice great diligence and pours over every word, remember "To Err is Human…"

Yes… I expect you to tattoo that phrase right across the back of your hand so that you never forget. (Oh, *okay*, in indelible marker, then…) No one is perfect and there will always be mistakes. Even if you were to have a flawless grasp of the English language, there will always be such things as typos. More importantly, after a certain point, we become so familiar with our work that our mind tricks our eye into reading what we expect to see on the page rather than what is really there. In all the years I've been writing seriously I have never picked up one of my stories without finding something that needs correction or adjustment. Even Piers Anthony has the philosophy that typos and spelling errors sprout on the page after the editing process.

Ensuring the most correct version of your work is presented to the public falls to you. There are many potential errors in a manuscript that is tens of thousands or even hundreds of thousands of words long: spelling, grammatical, continuity, factual… You will never catch all of those errors alone, though it will start with yourself. The most important step in polishing your writing is your own attitude: Your mantra needs to be "No work is a finished piece." In fact, even once I have submitted a piece of what I hope is polished writing for publication consideration, I always include in my cover letter the disclaimer that any suggestions for the story's improvement are welcome, regardless of how many times I have already gone over it.

The next step in polishing your work is read-through, after read-through, after read-through, but remember, each time you personally review your work your effectiveness diminishes. There are several ways around this:

- Have your friends—both writers and non-writers—do a read-through for you, noting any errors they notice or questions they might have. (This is to see if the common reader has any issues, as well as those more familiar with the craft.)
- Join a Writer's Group at your local library, bookstore, or on-line, where your work will be critiqued, in theory, by those more knowledgeable of grammar and structure.
- Hire an editor before you submit the work anywhere. (Not always financially feasible, but if you do be sure to research their credentials first.)

The publisher should have the work edited again on their end before publication, but sometimes things don't go as we expect. If that happens in your case, it is to be hoped you will have already caught the majority of serious errors with the above efforts. This isn't about questioning the abilities of the staff and freelancers employed by publishers these days, but it is about taking responsibility for your own work and recognizing everything can use improvement. There are a lot of aspiring writers out there and not nearly as many publishing opportunities, but with so much competition, extraordinary steps will help in getting your work noticed and minimizing the possibility of embarrassing mistakes for which the audience, be they publishers, reviewers, or the reading public, will look to attribute to you, not some faceless editor who "should have caught it in the first place."

Remember… To Err Is Human… and there is no such thing as a finished piece.

Flexibility Is A Virtue

(Originally published in the column If We'd Words Enough and Time)

A wise old author once imparted on me a gem of advice: No matter what, be flexible. Note, I said "wise old author," not "dirty old author." The flexibility is in our writing and our mindset, and there are several different dimensions to this advice.

Flexibility in Novels

Okay, so you have written the next great novel of our century and you have been fortunate enough — with hope — to find someone willing to take a look at it. Good for you, excellent, in fact. This is nearly as hard to do as writing the book to begin with, particularly in this day and age of "no unsolicited manuscripts" (for those of you new to the business, this means your manuscript doesn't have a pimp… sorry… agent!).

Now, when you send your manuscript off — unfailingly following the submission guidelines to the letter — you will include a cover letter. This is where your flexibility begins. Your first impulse will be to tell the extremely fortunate editor what a treasure they have before them. Resist… believe me… resist. What you need to do is thank them for taking the time to consider your work and let them know you would be open to any suggestions they might make that would improve the quality of the manuscript.

Some of you might be prepared to stalk off in a huff right now and say "No way! This is my masterpiece, it is whole and complete and immaculate." And that is all well and good, but you know what the editor is going to say, "Well, this isn't quite what I was looking for, and this passage here is a little rough, and my god! The typos, the grammar... Maybe we can work with it... but..." It's true, and that is if you are lucky. Always be humble when you are asking someone to have faith in your work. That is the hardest, yet most important aspect of the flexibility you will need to be a writer.

Think you can manage that? Good, because that is only the beginning. If you are fortunate enough to make it through negotiations and sign a deal (after being asked to rewrite half the book already) then your manuscript goes to the copyeditor and the nightmare begins for it is their job to take your efforts and pick them apart down to nearly the cellular level and rebuild. If you are fortunate, you will recognize a glimmer of your original work in there somewhere... eventually.

Okay, so I exaggerate, but only a bit. I have a friend who is an established author with multiple books under his belt with a major publisher. He had to add fifty pages to his manuscript before the editor would even consider an agreement—because there wasn't enough war in it. The publisher already had the first two books in this tetraology and they would have turned down the third book because they were bloodthirsty. My friend was flexible, in went fifty pages of war. My author friend's reasoning? He will add the fifty pages because it is a matter of paying his dues and securing his place, because if he does not compromise now, he will not be in a position to set terms later in his career. And this is an already established author. Imagine what is asked of the aspiring author.

Do not... I repeat... do NOT make a big stink about changes the publisher wants to make in your work. Very few of us have the bargaining power of Stephen King or Danielle Steel, and if we alienate the editors, we never will. If there is a problem with the revisions (as in it makes the story make absolutely NO sense whatsoever) then talk the matter over with them, but always in a cooperative manner.

Flexibility in Short Fiction and Other Venues

Another way for a writer to establish themselves is through the publication of short fiction, articles, and poetry in magazines and anthologies. Once again, your query letter will be your key to holding the editor's attention long enough for them to consider your work. The way to do this is not to be flashy (the last thing you want is for your cover letter to take attention away from your actual work), but to be respectful. One or two short paragraphs indicating what you are sending and expressing an interest in suggestions that will improve the work. They don't want to work with prima donnas, they have enough of them with the big names.

Since many anthologies and magazine issues are theme driven, it can be in your favor to query the editor, asking if there was anything in particular they were looking for that they did not receive. I know an author that did this for an anthology that was to be about the old west, he asked the editor and it turned out that of all the things that were received, not one of them dealt with the building of the railroad. My friend whipped something out and it made it in to the anthology.

This won't work every time, but by being flexible and willing to give the editors what they want, rather than what you want to give them, you build your prospects for being invited to other projects in the future.

Now That You're as Twisted as a Pretzel...

No matter what venue or genre you write in, being humble and accommodating—within reason—will improve your chances of getting a foothold in the writing world. Eventually, if you are fortunate, you will be in a position to set terms, but the easier you are to work with and the less arrogant you become, the smoother your path to literary immortality will be.

Rejection and the Tender-Hearted Youth

(Originally published in the column If We'd Words Enough and Time)

Last One Picked for the Team

Do you have faith in yourself? Do you see the merit of your work? Well… then everyone else will too, won't they? Unfortunately, this is not an if-then situation. One of the greatest hurdles in the literary world is the constant, guaranteed threat of rejection. How you deal with this rejection will plot the course of your literary career for all time.

So, I guess the first question is: How bad do you want to be an author? You noticed I said author and not writer, right? Of course, you did. This is an important distinction. The moment you put pen to paper—or fingers to keys, or stylus to touch screen, or… you get the picture—you *are* a writer. The transition takes place with publication. When your name is on the professionally printed page the transformation begins and "writer" becomes "author." A heady sensation, though not as glamorous as you might think… but that is a topic for another time.

Make no doubt, the distinction between writer and author is an important one, for there are those who—though some of us cannot fathom it—have no desire to become the latter, whose entire goal in life is to content themselves with the wonder of being the former, all for their own sublime enjoyment. For the sake of perpetuating this article, let's assume "author" is your ultimate goal.

Maintaining a healthy perspective is the key... and cultivating at least a kernel of thick-skinned hubris. Without it you will scatter like dust on the wind after your first dozen or so rejections.

Dear John...

Rejection... even the word is abhorrent to us. It cuts us to the quick and lays bare our insecure hearts. Fear is not the little death... rejection is. It cultivates doubt and discouragement until we question our own value, the merit of our work. With each rejection a tiny part of our confidence dies... if we let it.

I have forced myself to view each rejection or negative review with a ruthless clarity. First, how readily — and honestly — can I refute what they say? If I cannot, then I would do well to listen with an open mind and learn from their observations. Do they complain of things that can be easily fixed? Is this the first time I have heard this particular criticism, or is it a recurring theme that uncovers something I must learn to work on in my writing? If I am going to court comments, I must extract every bit of value from them. Nothing is a finished work. The world, in every aspect, is in a constant state of change. Our work is a microcosm of the world.

Ultimately, the most common cause of rejection or other negative response — those reactions having nothing to do with the technical aspects of grammar, continuity, and construction — is personal preference. Not everything we write will appeal to all. It is not possible. Not only do we all look for different things in our reading, but we also bring to the experience different understandings. Some will be blind to our vision and death to the poetry of our words. That does not speak to our merit, only the observer's perception.

Always a Bridesmaid

"This is not quite the exceptional work I am able to add to my crowded plate right now."

"This story belongs to the world... in one or two more drafts... but I cannot see it for what it is: a published work."

Quite a blow to one's "golden child"... With each strike, a bit of the gold leaf flakes off, revealing the foundation as less-than-priceless. These are two of the most devastating responses I have ever received on my own work. Without a doubt, a humbling experience. And yet, if I allow myself to be blinded by the rejection, I have defeated myself.

A knee-jerk reaction is to accept the judgment without analyzing it. What is the standpoint these people are responding from? Is it personal preference? Is it with an eye to profit or marketability? Is there a flaw I can work around? Our ability to change, to adapt, is one of our greatest strengths. This is as true in our writing as any other part of our existence.

Woo the world, entice them... use confidence and skill to convince them, but be true to yourself. Your opinion should not be lost to the challenge of changing theirs.

Red Pill or Blue Pill?

Which would you chose? In the realm of literary success, will you chose self-delusion? A fantasy realm where only your own opinion matters? Or will you chose a proactive role; seeing every response, positive or negative, as a gauge, a tool to hone your skill? Do you hold tight to your conviction that your work puts the classics to shame? Or will you give serious thought to the humble acknowledgement that yes, even your masterpicce needs a bit of polish—or complete revitalization—before the world can see its merit? My advice to you: grow that thick skin. Don't let them tear you down with their brutal words. Recognize that every rejection is but one opinion. Take what you can of value from it, but refuse the debasement of your worth. One man's opinion... ten men's opinion... even a hundred's, is still just that: an opinion. Listen to what they say, and how they say it, not to validate, but to cull the indifference and gather to you any observation that might nurture and hone your talent.

A Little Friendly Abuse

(Originally published as "Where Two or Three – Or Twenty – Are Gathered" in The Complete Guide To Writing Fantasy: The Author's Grimoire, by Dragon Moon Press)

Writing, they say, is a solitary endeavor.

I say it is a journey you make with your friends: those you write for, those you write about, and those who make it all come together by helping you figure out where you went wrong.

True, for the most part you sit yourself before your computer… or typewriter… or clay tablet… and pretend the world outside your head is not there, but for those writing with the hope of publication this is only one third of the process (refining the resulting manuscript and promoting the finished product being the other two legs of this triumvirate). With that in mind, it is my task to tell you about one of the writer's most valuable tools: the Writer's Group.

What Exactly Are We Talking About?

On the off chance that it might actually be there, I looked up *Writer's Group* in The Oxford English Dictionary and alas, though countless triviality, including that which follows somewhere after Muffle, has made it into those exalted pages, *Writer's Group* has not. The same went for Miriam-Webster's, and the Cambridge Dictionary. Surprising considering you can't turn around without encountering someone that wants to be a writer. Well, that just leaves me to define the term for myself.

I say Writer's Groups are meetings of passions, minds, and on occasion bodies. The one key and unifying factor of such groups is that they be attended by, of course, writers — aspiring, established, and every stage in between. While such meetings can have varying objectives (which I will soon discuss), the key element is a desire to write (that is the passion I reference above, so you can stop looking for the X-rating at the top of this chapter).

To Put a Fine Edge on It

While I am sure there are countless variations on Writer's Groups in the world, I am going to focus on three basic types (and please keep in mind, these labels are my own): The Social Club, the Crucible, and the Community. Every group I have ever been a part of or encountered has been some combination of these three elements.

The Social Club. When you are shopping around for a group of your own, it is important to be sure of both what you are looking for, and what you are getting into. Not every Writer's Group focuses on polishing the craft.

I know. What is the sense in that? Well, some people like to socialize. This process — especially for someone who sits alone in front of a monitor, pretending the outside world doesn't exist — is made easier when there is common ground. What that means for you is that though the majority of people on or in the group are writers, the craft of writing may not be the primary topic of discussion. Participation and structure in the Social Club are characteristically relaxed.

That is not to say that such groups serve no purpose. Not only are they a place to commiserate and unwind among those who can relate, but they are also a means of networking with those in different tiers of the industry, or a pool to be tapped into if you yourself are looking for someone with certain writing-related skills. Think of it as the grapevine for writers, or a community bulletin board.

The Crucible. Do you have a general idea what this one is going to be like? Yeah, you're right, as painful as it sounds... well, for your ego, anyway. This is the intense, no-nonsense Writer's Group. Think of it as diametrically opposed to the Social Club previously discussed. There is generally a great deal of regulation, a firm obligation to *give* as much, if not more feedback than you receive, and the bitter blow to your ego is not softened when they tear down your work and help you build it back up again, better, stronger than it was before.

The main factor of the Crucible is structure. The process is very formal and regimented, with certain plateaus to be reached and maintained before you can fully benefit from all the group has to offer. One such point being that those participating must meet an obligation to review and critique a set number of submissions before they are entitled to submit their own work into the process. Once they have reached this point they must maintain a quota of so many reviews in a given period if they wish to retain their submission privileges. Many times, though not always, emphasis is given to highlighting the flaws of a work that they may be eradicated and repaired, rather than on giving note to the positive attributes of a piece.

This might seem cruel and counterproductive to some, but it is not. The point is not to be brutal and unfair, but to be frank and exacting. For some writers constructive criticism is the best way to refine their work. They do not want to be told what works, because it does not need their attention. The purpose of the process is not to form a cheering section, but to gain productive feedback that will ultimately lead them as close to perfection as any of us is capable of. They already possess the confidence needed to succeed; what they need is an outside and objective perspective to hone their work to publishable quality.

The Community. This Writer's Group is about more than just honing skills, it is also about support and encouragement, celebrating successes and commiserating about rejections. This is a writing community that shares its knowledge of both publishing opportunities and the wisdom gained by experience, where topics generally gravitate around writing, though socializing and tangential conversations are not unheard of. A well-rounded environment that is writing-oriented but not narrow focused. The work is looked at as a whole: what works is praised and what doesn't is addressed. This is the middle ground between the two groups we have already discussed. It is for people becoming more serious about their writing, but lacking the knowledge, experience, or perhaps the confidence in their own work to take it to the next level. The community is about nurturing.

How Shall We Meet Again?

Generally there are three methods by which Writer's Groups are conducted: In-person, on-line, and by correspondence. These three methods are also known to cascade into numerous variations on the theme when put into practice, tailored to fit a group's particular needs. The structure of the group decides when and how often "meetings" take place.

In-person groups take place just about anywhere: members' homes, libraries, bookstores, diners... the possibilities are, as they say, endless. Depending on the venue, and the availability of the members, these groups generally meet weekly or monthly. To connect with one, visit the local community bulletin board or website, check the classifieds of the local weekly paper, or ask at the college campus, bookstore, or library nearest you.

One of the drawbacks of these groups is the experience level is generally uniform across the board, with everyone having very little knowledge about the technique of writing or experience with actually being published, or grossly unbalanced with the majority of members having little or no experience and one or two people being more advanced. In the first case the majority of the feedback received is going to be subjective, based on the readers' tastes, rather than on any firm understanding of why something works or what the industry is looking for. In most instances, critiques are vague and unproductive. In the second case, those who have little experience will benefit more from the feedback of those who have achieved some level of proficiency, while those with more experience will not get as much out of the group.

On-line groups are the most fluid. Conducted by means of message boards, live journals, blogs, newsgroups, list-serves, email, or any combination therein, their activity — while dependent on the participation of the members — is for the most part continuous. Its flexibility is in being able to participate when it suits your schedule. Also, because the web is far reaching, the experience levels are more divergent so everyone generally finds something of use in their own efforts.

Because of the diversity of the medium, the resources available to such groups can be more valuable than the member interaction itself. With endless links for writer's resources and submission sites and research pages easily passed from member to member for immediate access, this avenue of meeting has revolutionized Writer's Groups.

Also, the method in which you interact with the group can be chosen for the way that most suits you. Message boards, live journals, and blogs have features that can send an email alert to let you know when there has been activity on a particular topic, and newsgroups allow you to tailor your user preferences so that you receive posts by email as they are made, once a day by digest, or none at all, in which case you access them at your leisure via the newsgroup home page.

These are also the easiest to find, though you will have to try out a few before you find one that is a good fit. Check out the classified section of your favorite writers' magazine or run a web search on Writer's Groups. You will find literally millions of hits. All you will have to do is decide if you want one for writers in general, or one tailored to a specific genre or style that you write in. There are benefits to both.

The flaw of this method is volume. There are so many groups to choose from that it might be difficult at first to pin down one that suits both your needs and your personality. With some internet groups and boards activity is sporadic and not always helpful, with others the members participate with such enthusiasm your mailbox will literally overflow each day. Such can clearly be overwhelming, even if the dialogue is stimulating and resourceful. For the most part it is just a matter of moving on to another group until you find something you are comfortable with, but after a time the registering processes some groups require can be tedious and off-putting.

Once you have found your group, the next great hurdle is conflict among the members. Sometimes that can be more brutal in the faceless realm of the internet where typed words can be misinterpreted or filled with venom to a degree that would not necessarily happen in a face to face encounter. Such occurrences are inevitable; the mark of a good group is when they are the exception rather than the rule, and they are promptly defused by those running the show.

Correspondence groups are in a way a more personal interaction. Conducted by conventional mail, they can be an exchange between yourself and one other person, or a handful of people, but for the most part groups such as this are small and selective. This method most benefits those who are, for one reason or another, unable to travel to an in-person group and do not have readily available or dependable internet access.

Interaction in this case is restricted by delivery time. The frequency of exchange is determined by how quickly you receive and review the work, and how dependable the postal service is in returning it. (In theory, it would also be possible to use a fax to go back and forth in this method of "meeting," but given the variable quality of fax print-outs, this may or may not be a good idea.) This method can be supplemented by phone conversations, though depending on the distance, this can grow costly.

To find others who are interested in such an exchange, look to friends, family, or the classified portion of writers' magazines. Whichever of these methods you choose to employ, take care to protect your work. Any time you exchange ideas or material with an acquaintance you are taking a risk. Whether you know the individual or not, there are those who have no qualms against claiming work or ideas that are not their own. It is horrible, but true.

The Creative Approach: Alternatives to Structured Writing Groups

As I touched upon earlier, for some of you, where you live, the type of equipment you have, or other physical or time constraints may prevent you from taking advantage of the more standard Writer's Group options, which are, as discussed, in-person and via the internet website or news group. One alternative I've already mentioned is critiquing by correspondence. Now I will review a few more supplementary options.

Writers' Seminars or Workshops

Run a search on the internet, or pick up a writers' magazine, and you will find pages and pages of sites or ads for Writers' Seminars and Workshops, ranging from anywhere to a weekend or several weeks in length. Some are extremely discriminating, others are open to all. Almost all of them have a hefty participation fee.

Programs such as Clarion, which holds workshops around the nation and even in Europe, and Odyssey, the annual Fantasy Writing Workshop run by Jeanne Calevos—former senior editor with Bantam Doubleday Dell—in Manchester, New Hampshire, are by acceptance only. Think of them as literary boot camp. Or crash-course inductions into the professional literary world. These are intensive programs organized and run by industry professionals to prepare those whose work is almost, but not quite publishing quality. There are only a limited number of openings and they are allotted for those whose sights are set on a literary career. Your work is evaluated and you are then allowed into the program, or refused. These workshops can be brutal and costly in both time and money, but they also provide an intense writing evaluation and seminar geared toward honing your talent. They will take your work and tear it down to the ground, and then show you how to put it back together stronger than it was before. Courses are taught by established authors and experienced editors, those who already have an intimate knowledge of the field you are attempting to break into. Courses such as these will not coddle you, but if you let them, they will improve your abilities and understanding of what it is to be a published author.

For those who view their writing as a more casual passion, there are numerous other workshops where the process of admittance is less stringent, where those with the fee and a desire to improve their writing are welcome. The structure of such workshops is more discussion panels and mini-seminars that for the most part do not need to be signed up for—though there are exceptions to this. Such workshops are generally a weekend, or perhaps a week in length, and attendees set their own schedule based on the topics on offer and which they think they will most benefit from. Again, presenters and lecturers are professionals in the field, established authors, editors, publicists and such.

Another draw of these writers' workshops is the networking opportunities. The organizers not only set up programming to help writers polish their work, but they also arrange formal pitch sessions and meet-and-greet receptions.

Literary Conventions

I'm going to include something under this venue that might have some of you looking at me cockeyed, but among the ranks of Writer's Groups I include the literary convention. On mostly any given weekend of the year there is a literary convention taking place somewhere in the world and, in the world of fandom there are convention gypsies. Though not every panel discussion at such conventions is about the craft of writing, enough of them are that they would be a benefit to someone wanting to polish their abilities. There is a lot to be gained from listening to your favorite authors explain how they approach their craft.

In addition to such panels, some conventions have actual writers workshops, which can take two different tacks: A panel of established authors and editors evaluating pre-submitted works, pointing out the strengths and weaknesses and offering constructive criticism on how to improve the story; or, an informal panel where the moderator has prepared a series of mini-exercises to show ways to advance your writing. While the duration of such workshops is generally only two to three hours, the benefits can be innumerable. Most weekly and monthly writers groups do not offer the feedback of professionals in the field, especially editors, the very people you most notably need to reach and please.

Who Am I to Talk? Let Me Tell You...

You may ask what qualified me to write on this topic, to educate you on this phenomenon. Well, at the time I am writing this, I am a part of no less than five on-line Writer's Groups, all of them some variation of what I've outlined above. Most notably, though is the fact that I founded and have been running for the past eight years Yesterday's Dreamers, a Writer's Group on Yahoo! Groups, While there is absolutely no way I've seen it all, I've seen a lot!

For those of you who have tried what I have mentioned above and met with little success, or those whose situations make it difficult to take advantage of my advice, I would make one more suggestion: start your own Writer's Group. Decide what you are looking for and find others of a like interest. This isn't easy, but it can be done. For myself, I was already a published author before I even knew what a newsgroup was. I discovered them as a useful tool during a literary convention when I was promoting my work. That made getting started easy for me; all I had to do was set out a sign-up sheet. People interested in me and what I had to say put down their email address and they received an invitation to the newsgroup. Using this method I have gathered people around me not only interested in writing, but also interested in fantasy and science fiction, which is what I primarily write. On top of that, I also had the benefit of starting the initial relationship with about ninety percent of my members in person. Because we met through conventions, we even occasionally reunite in real time.

Not everyone is going to have such an opportunity for start-up. What you can do is begin with people you already know that share your interest and desire to improve, then move from there to place one of those ads I've been mentioning in either the local paper or writers' magazines.

When starting your own group—on-line or in person—keep in mind that structure, organization, and discipline will be the key to smooth operation. Not only does my group's home page clearly state my intentions for the group, but each time we have a new member join I formally greet them and outline how the group works. We are currently up to sixty-eight members, many of whom are only lurkers (silent and don't generally contribute, but as they haven't quit, they must get something out of the group). There is a core of about twenty to twenty-five members who regularly contribute to discussions and a handful more who occasionally comment on a topic. Because the majority signed up at literary conventions we have a nice mix of experience levels and everyone benefits.

Decide what you want for yourself and what kind of group you would like to have. For an in-person group, approach a local library, bookstore, school, or diner, any quiet place where there is space, chairs, and someone in charge willing to work out the details with you, and gather your group.

If you are going for an on-line group, there are plenty of list-serves, newsgroup servers, and message boards to choose from. All require some form of registration, and naturally some are better organized than others. Look for one that does not clutter your posts with ads, and that has a dependable reputation.

Once you pick your method of meeting, decide on a schedule (if applicable) and what your objectives are. For me, I intended that my newsgroup would be mainly a support structure; a place where writers could share opportunities and successes, and ask specific questions regarding the mechanics of writing generally related to snags they have hit in their own work. This has served us well and has kept most people interested, without bogging everyone down with stories to read.

Because some people needed a fresh perspective on their work, and feedback based on experience, we also run a critique group by email, separate, but still linked to the newsgroup. The precept for that is simple: everyone submits a story, the names are stripped off, the anonymous selections are sent to everyone participating that round, and everyone is free to comment without being self-conscious about commenting on a friend's story or worrying about everyone else knowing which one is theirs. The only guidelines they are given is to be positive and constructive in their comments, pointing out both the strengths and weaknesses in a piece. The group takes a month and half to read through all of the submissions before sending in their feedback, and then the cycle starts again.

In this way my Writer's Group has the flexibility that those who want or need feedback receive it, and those who just require a sounding board can sit back and enjoy the discussions.

Everything in Moderation

Whether you are joining someone else's group, or starting your own, policing the members is very important. Knowing when to speak up and when to sit back and let a situation fade on its own isn't easy, but it is going to come up. Any time you bring two or more people together there is potential for disagreement, especially in a group as opinionated as writers. Add ego to that and eventually worlds will collide. If you are moderating or just caught in the crossfire, tact is your most powerful weapon. Redirect the conversation, or intercede in a way that reminds the combatants that everything is a matter of opinion and the important thing is not to confuse different with wrong. If diplomacy doesn't work, take the offenders off to the side (physically or metaphorically) and explain that if they cannot come to an agreement they need to restrict themselves to commenting peaceably on topics unrelated to the disagreement and take the argument outside the group. Anyone who continues to be a disruptive force ultimately must be asked to leave. It is harsh, but necessary at times.

Remember, regardless of the type of group you are in Writer's Groups are about connecting, support, sharing, and improving your ability. Politics are best left by the wayside.

Anthologies
The New Magazines

Well, not really, but in the scheme of a writer's career, they serve the same purpose. See, it takes a long time to write a novel. Takes even longer to get it published, unless you are very lucky — or not very picky. That can be a problem when it comes to keeping your name in the public eye. Supplementing your efforts with short fiction is the way around that, assuming you are comfortable writing short, not everyone is. It is a skill worth cultivating if you are serious about being a published author.

In the heyday of magazines, a writer could build and sustain a respectable career, not to mention a steady pay check by submitting to that market. Unfortunately, the market is shrinking. There just isn't enough audience for all of the subscription publications out there, particularly when there is so much of their content available via the web. Anthologies have become more prevalent, filling both the readership's desire for a ready source of portable short fiction, and the writer's need for a market of such.

A Brief Primer

As with magazines, anthologies come in many varieties. Some are themed, others cater to a particular audience, and yet others feature the best of... well, whatever. Let's look at what all of that means:

Unthemed. Writers submit on any topic and there is no unifying factor from story to story, other than that they are in the same collection. This means freedom for the writer, as they are not restricted in what they submit, but not as appealing to the reader because there is the real possibility they will not be interested in all the stories. With unthemed, the audience is more likely to be influenced by the names in the book.

Themed. Well, this is pretty self-explanatory. This is a collection of stories that have an overall theme connecting them. The theme can be broad, or very, very specific, but it serves to unify the content so that it is targeting a particular market with which that theme is popular. Basically, it means the reader is more likely to pick it up because they know what to expect, in general, from each story. Examples of themes are Love-At-First-Sight, Vampires, Pirates and Magic. Yeah, pretty much anything. The benefit of this type of anthology is that readers may be drawn by the topic, even if they are unfamiliar with the authors.

Shared Universe. I know… *what*? This is a kind of very specific themed anthology where the author must write in someone else's established universe. Mostly you see these as media tie-ins (universes based on television or movie franchises), but occasionally you will see them based on gaming systems or popular novels by other authors. These collections are most likely—but not always—invitation-only and require the author to either already be conversant with the universe, or adherence to a series bible that familiarizes the writer with the relevant details before they start writing. Basically, you are playing in someone else's playground. It can be good for getting your name out there, but can also limit you when it comes to writing your own original work, which may not be as well received if the readership has come to expect other material from you.

Best Of. Mostly this is here just so I know I'm doing a thorough job. We all hope to be included in one of these someday. Someone else generally decides. Whoever is putting the collection together decides on their source and the parameters of the collection and then they comb through all the works published that fit those guidelines. It might be the best of the year, the best of a particular magazine or genre, or the best of a particular author. Consequently, this is a reprint type of anthology. In some cases the editors find the material on their own; in others you or your publisher might have the opportunity to send in a collection that contains your work for consideration. Mostly, you have no control over this one, but yes... we can all dream!

Now all of this only covers content. With anthologies there is another way of classifying them that we should look at. That deals with the terms of submitting.

Open Submissions. This is where a call is made public and anyone can submit as long as they follow the parameters set out by those putting the collection together. There is a lot of competition from hopefuls like yourself.

Semi-Open Submissions. The editors make a limited public announcement being very specific where it appears. Less competition, but also potentially less opportunity.

Invitation Only. Well yeah, it's just what it says. The editors hand-select specific writers they would like to include in the collection — or have writers recommended to them. With this type it is about who you know... or who knows (of) you. Acceptance is not guaranteed, but is more likely, depending on the editor and if they have ordered exactly enough writers for the number of stories they want to include, or if they invited more than needed and must select from among them.

Reprint. This is generally a variation on both Invitation Only and Themed combined. Basically an editor or publisher decides they want to publish a particular collection (say, on Lovecraftian Horror or Dog stories... just saying). They will go through a bunch of published fiction that fits their chosen parameters and then attempt to secure the reprint rights from the author or the previous publisher, depending on who holds the rights (assuming the story isn't in the public domain, which is quite possible).

Competition. These may or may not have an entry fee. I tend to stay away from those that do, just because there are enough out there without them that I figure, why pay? Competition collections are usually incidental to a particular writing contest. Meaning, you enter the contest to win the prize—usually monetary—and the anthology is just a small part of that prize. Competitions are generally governed by theme or genre and often have restrictions as to who can submit based on experience level. In other words, if you have too many pro credits, you might be excluded, so check all of the contest guidelines carefully. However, if you haven't made a break into the industry, this might be a good way to do it as many of the contests are high-profile and can serve to quickly propel you out of obscurity... at least initially. (After that it is up to you to make sure you stay visible.)

How to Find Them

This is the easy part, believe it or not. These days it seems everyone is putting together anthologies, particularly in the small press markets, but even with the major houses.

Why? Well, to capitalize on the market. If you are trying to draw an audience it is much more productive to tap the fan base of multiple writers than just one or two.

It used to be anthologies were either school books, best of, or reprint collections, and there were relatively few of them. These days they abound. Just go to the internet and you will find hundreds of prospects... and those are just the ones open to everyone. There are various websites that specialize in listing anthology and other publishing opportunities. Most notable is www.ralan.com, but there are others out there.

Whatever you do, be cautious and research publishers you are considering submitting to. Be sure you know their reputation, what they offer, and what rights they are requiring. I also recommend looking for other books they have done to see the quality of both the writing and the production.

Another option—presuming you have contacts in the editing/publishing world—ask. I know… seems obvious, but did you think of it? Not everyone would. Asking around though, can't hurt, and it might just get you an opportunity to submit to collections that aren't necessarily open to the general public.

Summing Up

I could go on and on about anthologies. After all, I've barely touched on them here, but the truth is, I could—and likely will—write a book on the topic. For now, though, this is just to introduce you to the possibilities.

In the time of the vanishing, or at best, uncertain magazine market, anthologies are a gold-mine of opportunity. They get your name out into the public eye, and—with hope—keep it there while you are working on longer works of fiction. They serve as both career-building and promotional tools, as well as another source of periodic income—again, with hope. If short fiction is a part of your skill-set, by all means, this is a venue you should consider pursuing.

On the Size of Fishes and Ponds
Your Place in the Publishing World

I have to tell you—though I probably don't *need* to—that you have not picked an easy passion. Or a solitary one, for that matter. You are in plentiful company in your desire to be published. (Let's face it, if you only wanted to write you wouldn't be reading this book.) The important part of this conversation is that the proportions of hopeful writers to publishing opportunities are not very favorable. Given that, I think we should talk options.

Yes. You have options. You might not like all of them, but then, that's another conversation entirely.

Option 1: Write just to write. (I know… most of you are saying, *what's the point?*) Getting published takes a combination of things: skill, patience, perseverance, connections, and pure, dumb luck are the primary ones. Your potential for getting published decreases exponentially the more of those you have missing from your toolbox. If you are not prepared to be dedicated to the proposition, don't set your goal on seeing your name in print. Getting your clichéd foot in the door (and keeping it there) takes a lot of time, effort, and frustration. Be ready for that or don't even bother to knock.

Option 2: Self-publishing. (Here's where I say, *what's the point? No… really, it is.*) You have to ask yourself what the true focus of your goal is. If you want to be published just so you can have a book with your name on it to put on your shelf or give out at Christmas, okay, this may be a viable option for you. If you want to have a career in publishing, consider carefully if this is the best way for you to go. It could work great for you, or it could be literary suicide.

Want to know why I say this? Might as well, since we are here. Most publishing professionals will not give serious consideration to a work that has been self-published. Yes, there are exceptions, but those are precisely that. The majority of fiction that is produced by self-publishing is not of professional quality: either the writing or the book production. The reason for this? Most writers do not have the skills or knowledge to put together a professional quality book. When you go to a vanity press one of the ways they make money is to get the author to do the majority of the work. They make it seem like they are giving you creative control, but in truth they are working every angle they can to get you to do the job you are paying them to do. Unless you work in publishing or a similar field you just don't have the skill set to know what makes good cover art, or back cover copy; you probably wouldn't recognize poor design or indifferent editing. These are all characteristics endemic of self-published books.

Now that is just looking at the technical aspects of publishing your book. There is a more fundamental reason why self-publishing could hurt you. It is the matter of paying your dues. No. Not talking about a pro organization here or anything like that, but self-publishing can send the message that you are impatient enough not to try your luck with everyone else that has had to claw their way into the industry based on merit. Some would see it as a lack of dedication. If it was too much effort for you to go through conventional methods, it implies you either couldn't be bothered to earn your place among the ranks of published authors, or you weren't good enough to. Now whether or not either of those opinions are valid is irrelevant, we're talking implications here, not facts. Bare bones, it's going to look like you bought your way into the game.

There are some specific exceptions to this. It is unfortunate, but this stigma seems to apply predominantly to adult fiction. When it comes to picture books, comics, graphic novels, and role-playing games it is virtually expected you will self-publish until you have proven yourself a viable commodity. There are also cases of established authors self-publishing their backlist once rights have reverted to keep the titles alive.

I am not saying self-publishing isn't a viable way to go... but I am saying consider everything carefully, do your homework, be ready to put in time, effort, and/or cash to make that dream happen if you go it on your own. Not only will you need to do—or hire out—all the production work, but also manage the business and promotional side. It isn't enough to produce a book, you have to have a plan for how to distribute and market it.

Option 3: Online. Often there isn't any money in it, but publishing via online markets can be a way past the dreaded slush pile. This venue offers online magazines, eBooks, and articles or fiction for dedicated websites featuring such things. Some pay, some don't. When there is money involved it is usually just a token, so you have to decide what the publishing credit is worth for you. The standards for this venue are not lower, but the opportunities are more plentiful and less market-driven. Online is a good way to build a personal bibliography that may just get you a bit more notice in more traditional markets, depending on the site where you are published.

Option 4: Magazines. Some people write strictly short fiction. The typical market for such things has in the past been magazines. They reach—one would hope—a wide and dedicated audience generally anywhere from one to twelve times a year, depending on the magazine circulation. Magazines are good for reaching a target audience, as well as for increasing the visibility of your name. In addition to that, the high-level magazines at least are automatically sifted for award nominations for the major genre awards each year, as well as best-of collections, whereas most anthologies only come to the attention of the nominating board or best-of editors if a copy is sent to them by the publisher.

Unfortunately, most magazines lately, even those well-established and considered major publications, are an unstable market. With the internet affecting subscription and sales numbers many of the smaller and even some of the larger magazines have gone under. Because of this, competition is fierce, making it difficult to get an acceptance. Of course, that means rejection turn-around time is generally swift. You can make a name for yourself publishing strictly in magazines, but there will be a lot of effort and waiting.

It bears noting for the novelists out there, some magazines have been known to run longer works as serials. Not as prevalent these days, but something to look into.

Option 5: Small Press. By far this is the market where most authors find recognition for their work. The primary reason for this? There are a greater number of small presses than there are major publishing houses, and small press is more driven by niche markets rather than marketing (sales) trends. This is a relatively new development in the publishing industry, mostly in the past ten to fifteen years, mostly made possible by the advent of POD — or print on demand technology. Because of this development it became possible for the smaller publishers to build their catalogue without the expense of printing and storing masses of books. This gives them the luxury of putting more titles in print and leaving them there for longer, taking the long view on profitability.

The primary draw-back of small press? The 'small' applies to virtually every aspect of the business: staff, profit, promotions, budget, etc. Since the money is not there, normal production tasks like editing, design, and proofreading are often handled by one person, or freelancers. This can introduce a variable quality to the finished product, as well as an unpredictable publication schedule. (Remember what I said about patience and dedication.) In addition to that, there is virtually no budget for marketing. With a small press it is a guarantee that the author will have to take a very active part in promoting the work; of course, in my experience, it doesn't matter what size your publisher is, you should put maximum effort behind promoting your book anyway. Even assuming the publisher has a marketing campaign, who has a more vested interest in your work? The answer certainly isn't the person in charge of promotions. Still, a writer can do very well in the small press market, often having a longer publication life and more flexibility in content than would be found in more traditional publishing.

Option 6: Major Houses. What do they say? Go for the gold? Maybe. Or maybe not. As is most often the case, even if you are fortunate enough to be picked up by a major publisher, you end up with gold leaf, not bullion.

Why? They gamble, but only penny ante. They take a chance on a small portion of new authors, but the majority of their lists are comprised of proven money makers. How? Well, say you sold your book to a major house. You are an unknown quantity. Most likely your writing was decent and you had the solid luck of landing on the editor's desk with a story line that hit the current marketing trend. They put minimal budget behind your book, set you up with the bare basics on promotions, and then they sit back and see how you sell. If you do, you've dodged the bullet. If you do but not to the standard they are looking for, you get cut, your book goes out of print, and they likely won't accept another manuscript.

So, why do people aspire to this? Well, it helps to have a big, established name behind you, even if they don't do very much; there is the chance that you will be that break-out hit; and whatever else they do or do not have, major houses have distribution. Face it, if you are going to hit it big it is more likely to happen with a major publisher; but if you are more interested in longevity and the opportunity to build your name, this might not be the place for you.

Summing Up

Basically, when it comes down to it, you have to decide what you want out of this dedicated hobby you've chosen. How much effort is it worth to you? What are you willing to gamble? No matter which publishing option you choose—with the exception of the first one—it is going to take time, effort, patience, and dedication on your part. My best advice: don't sit back and wait for anything to happen. Figure out what you want and work toward that. No one else is going to do it for you. If you don't want it bad enough... you never really wanted it at all.

Something More Than a Thick Skin

You know, many beginning writers, once they've reached the stage of having something to push—yes, I said push, because you better believe that all of us who aspire to or have accomplished that vaunted goal of "published," seek to addict the masses to our particular works; but back to my point—many of those just getting started believe the worst thing writers must defend themselves against is the brutality of rejection and the tedium of waiting. I wish I could tell you they were right.

Publishing is a business.

Businesses are fraught with pitfalls. Shall we take a look at some of those you should look out for?

In the Market for a Bridge?

No one likes to think they might be taken advantage of (I know, common sense), but if you aren't familiar with publishing it is way too easy for this to happen. Heck, there are even a plethora of ways for this to happen.

Theft of Intellectual Property. Once you develop an idea it is yours. Unfortunately, the moment anyone else becomes aware of that idea, there is the potential of it being stolen. If the idea is in your head, there isn't much you can do about it. If you have the idea down on paper you might be able to make a legal case—*might*. Assuming the idea in question—or more to the point, the other person's success with your idea—is worth the prospect of a court battle you will need to establish (or try to, anyway) that the original concept was yours. Sadly, even with documentation, this is not always possible and the best you can often hope for is to reach a settlement... and walk away from your idea. To protect yourself against this, limit where, how, and with whom you share your concept. Among family and close friends you are *most likely* safe, but online and among casual acquaintances you might want to refrain from discussion.

Plagiarism. This is pretty much the same as above, only it generally refers to when someone tries to pass off as their own, in whole or in part, the published works of another person. The first step in protecting yourself against this possibility is to file your works with the copyright office. This can easily be done on line and is not very expensive. Another method of questionable effectiveness is what is called a poor man's copyright. This is when you mail yourself a copy of your manuscript by federal mail and file the unopened package away. In theory, the date stamp of the cancelled postage establishes an irrefutable point of ownership. As I said, it is a theory. I am told this is not ironclad, but it helps, particularly if you also have research and development notes.

Unfortunately, there is not much else you can do to guard against this; it is more a matter of watching for it once it becomes a potential threat. With shorter works it would likely be your responsibility to pursue action against this manner of theft; with novels and such, the publisher—and their lawyer—is the one to bring action, on your behalf, against the party in question as it is their commodity as long as they hold the rights.

Vanity/Subsidy Press. I've already talked about this some. Basically, these people are out to make money. They don't care about the quality of the book so much as the quantity of the titles they can produce... and how much of your money they can extract from you and the other hopefuls (and/or impatients). At best they will charge you every step of the way for every service, even those they manage to get you to do for them. At worse they will bind you in a contract—yes, they have contracts—that will tie up your rights for as much as the next ten years!

If you go this route, do your research. Not just into the press you are considering giving your money to, but also into the production process. Learn how to put a good, professional book together so that you can tell if you are getting your money's worth. And if there is a contract, be sure to have it looked at by someone knowledgeable (preferably a lawyer, but if not, at least someone familiar with publishing contracts).

As a side note, for those who write short fiction or poetry; if someone accepts your work for inclusion in a collection and 1) does not offer payment for the work, and 2) requires you to buy your personal copy, that is also vanity press.

When the Professionals Aren't

Now, the previous section just touches on those people consciously attempting to rip you off. Sadly, that is not all we risk in this venture. You need to educate yourself, which I presume you are more than willing to do considering you not only purchased this book... but you've read it this far!

In the days before the internet this was much harder for writers to do. There were a few books, and word of mouth, but mostly everyone took their chances and learned things the hard way. No excuse for that now. On the internet you can find virtually anything about anyone, pun intended. Before you approach any prospective publisher—or editors, agents or publicists, for that matter—do your homework! Run a search on the company name, look for individuals that have done business with them, see if there are any gripes against them. How visible are they on the internet? How professional is their presence? Do they have a reputation?

One of the best sites on the web for this is Preditors and Editors (http://pred-ed.com/) a free website that maintains an extensive listing of publishers and individuals/businesses related to the industry. Mostly only the basics are included: the publisher's address, what they publish, if they are still a viable market, and if they are recommended or not. However, the older entries can be somewhat extensive as they are continually updated as information is submitted to those that maintain the site, but generally they are a paragraph long or less. If anyone reports problems such as matters of ethics, payment, or communication, all of that is listed as well. There are also a variety of similar sites run by individuals, authors, and professional organizations, so be sure to check several sources for as complete an understanding as possible.

In addition to third-party sources, be sure to visit the publisher's website. It can tell you a lot about how professional they are. Also, if possible, take a look at the books they produce: the cover art, the interior design, the quality of the writing. Ask yourself if you would be pleased to have your name on the finished product. Look for information on distribution, where applicable, and terms.

Things to Look For In a Publisher

What is their distribution? A good publisher will be carried by at least one of the major distributors, which for fiction are Ingram and Baker and Taylor. Now, it is important to know that there are two types of accounts publishers can have with either of these companies: distribution, which means third parties can order stock through the distributor; and wholesale; which means the distributor will warehouse stock of the publisher's titles and supply them to the major chains. Small press generally only have distributor accounts.

Do they publish what you write? This is common sense; you don't go to an erotica/romance publisher if you are selling a cookbook and you don't try and interest a young adult publisher in an adult military science fiction.

What are their terms? I cover this more in depth in the next section, but basically check out the websites for the professional writers organizations for an idea of what standard terms are so you can tell if the publisher you are considering offers fair terms. They should not be too restrictive and there should be no concessions to the publisher after rights revert.

Does the publisher have a visible and professional presence on the web and in the market place? My first publisher was hardly even known by their authors, let alone the public. Small isn't necessarily bad, but visible is important. At the very least you should be able to find their titles on the major third-party internet sales sites like Amazon and Barnes and Noble.

Does the publisher promote and market their titles, beyond maintaining their own website? Now I've already mentioned that the author cannot and should not depend on this even if a publisher does have a marketing department, but it is important to know that they actively stand behind their product and make some effort to promote. You can tell if they do by checking their staff listing on their website or calling up their office and asking to speak to someone in the promotions department. You can also search for ads, listings, and such on the web or in magazines.

Is the product the publisher produces professional? You might have to invest in a book or two, but it is worth it to see if the publisher takes pride in the quality of their books or is just trying to get as many titles out as possible so they can make an accumulative profit.

Are their authors happy? Hard to know without talking with them, unless the recommended web search turns up any dirt, but something to consider.

Things to Look For in a Contract

What rights are they requesting? Industry standard is print (paperback, hardcover, or both), electronic, and worldwide English language rights. Any other rights you grant the publisher (audio, media, foreign language, etc) are at your discretion and should include a provision for what you would be paid should those rights come into play. You do have the right to request certain rights be removed from the contract, or to negotiate the terms by which they might be granted.

Are the rights exclusive, nonexclusive, or a mix of the two? Industry standard for novels is three years exclusive, with rights reverting upon written request, generally within 30 to 90 days of notice. This allows the publisher to recoup their production costs and sell any remaining stock before the rights revert. (They will often offer the author the opportunity to purchase any remaining copies themselves at a discount.) For short fiction, the publisher might request either one-year exclusive, followed by a period of nonexclusive rights for the above same reasons, depending on if the venue is a collection or a magazine. For reprinted material the terms should always be nonexclusive, as the work has already been previously published.

What payment is offered? There is no industry standard here. Possible payment methods depend on the level of the publisher and the type of publication. You can expect to see any combination of the following: advance (against estimated royalties), royalties, flat-fee, per-word, contributors' copies, and author discount (anywhere from 40 to 60%, generally). If a print and electronic version of the work is produced, the royalty rate on the electronic version is usually higher than the print version due to lower production costs.

What is the payment schedule? Industry standard is every six months to a year, with royalty statements provided quarterly, though there is as much variation here as there is in the actual form the payment takes. Some publishers even report and pay royalties monthly, though this is rare. With short fiction, depending on the type of publication, payment is either made in advance, upon publication, or as a royalty per above if the work is appearing in an anthology.

What terms have been laid out for rights reversion? As mentioned above, rights revert after a set number of days from receipt of the written request once the time obligation outlined in the contract has been met. It is up to the publisher's discretion if they will allow early rights revision before the obligation has been met.

Summing Up

Now I'm sure you know what I'll say right now… there is no way I've covered *everything* you need to know here. Not only would it fill a book all on its own, but I'm also sure that I haven't encountered every single stumbling block there is. The best I can tell you is to educate yourself in every way you can. Ask questions — of people or on the net — do research, and pay attention! There are good publishers, okay publishers, bad publishers, crooked publishers, and just plain incompetent ones, try and figure out which is which *before* you commit!

Unfortunately, there are plenty of things you are likely not going to find out until you start working with the publisher one-on-one. Things like, do they communicate in a timely manner? Do they pay royalties on schedule? Do they meet publication schedules? Do they remember details of agreements made post-contract? No publisher is going to be perfect; the best you can do is avoid the bad ones where you can and try someone else when the time comes if you can't.

Promoting For the Beginner

(Originally published as Let the World Know You're There: Promoting For The Beginning Author in The Graveline, the newsletter of the Garden State Horror Writers)

I've written and talked about this many times, but it bears repeating: finishing the book is not the end of an author's job. Neither is getting it under contract… or receiving your print or eBook copies. Unless, of course, that was your only goal.

Ask yourself what are you in this for? Is it just to add "author" to your list of accomplishments? Is it to have a display piece for your shelf? Maybe for some… but not generally. You want to share your stories, you want people to know your name, you want—as we all can't help but want to some degree—to hit the bestseller list and reap the lovely check that entails.

Word of advice… DON'T do it for the money. Maybe it will come, maybe it won't, but it will definitely demoralize you starting out if you expect four-figure checks. I've gotten those… there's always a decimal point in the middle.

I'm not saying it isn't possible for your writing to be lucrative and successful.

I'm saying it takes a lot of hard work… and not a little luck.

I've been a published author for nine years, I've graduated to five figure checks… if you count the two after the decimal. And excuse my frankness, but I've worked my ass off to get here. It's isn't easy.

Whether your credits are print, eBook, novels, anthology, or magazine contributions, it is your responsibility as an author to promote that work. You can't assume anyone else will. It would be nice, but the reality is usually otherwise. Who gets the most attention? The person standing on the sidelines watching and waiting quietly, or the loudmouth waving and jumping around?

Okay... maybe you don't want to be the loudmouth, either... but you can toot that horn and sing your praises — within reason — without making an annoyance out of yourself. How will people know to look for your work if they've never heard a thing about it?

My second bit of advice... promote yourself as an author, rather than just focusing on any one work. Books are transitory, they go out of print, they are overshadowed by new books in the audience's attention; magazines are fleeting as well, with another issue out relatively soon after. What you want if you are building a literary career is for the audience to know YOUR name, the rest will come after... if you do your job right.

The internet alone is a wealth of promotional opportunities, mostly free but for a little time, so I'll focus there for now.

Blogs. Just about everyone has a blog these days. They talk about what they ate, where they went, and what pissed them off that day. And people read it. Just think how productive your own efforts could be if just one day a week you posted news about your releases, your upcoming appearances, your writing process... You never know who will read that and go to check out what you've done.

Official Websites. As soon as you have credits to your name start one. Simple, but professional. There are programs you can use to create your own site, or freelancers out there who can put one together for you for a fee. Showcase yourself, post news, update as frequently as possible with author appearances or new releases, but have a presence.

Social Media. Twitter, Facebook, etcetera, etcetera, etcetera… there are tons of new and established social media venues from the general to the specific that you can utilize to reach your target audience. Once you're set up, most of them are relatively easy to maintain. The cool thing from a promotional standpoint… most of these can be linked with Twitter or your blog so that you get three times the exposure for one posting, and in theory you are reaching a different audience with each one.

Book Sites. As with the social media, there are a bunch of sites that cater to book-readers, and most if not all of them have some feature you can activate that give you extra *umph* as an author. Even if you don't frequent these sites make sure you establish some kind of presence.

Network. Whether in person or via online groups, this is vital. Make an effort to meet professionals in the industry. I belong to the New Jersey Authors Network, the Garden State Horror Writers, and Broad Universe. Each one has something different to offer me as an author. Doesn't matter which group you join as long as it is active, productive, and you can meet others like yourself who are trying to get started, those with the same interests. Share what you've learned, listen to what they have figured out, and keep your ear open to publishing and promoting opportunities. Conventions are a great opportunity for this, as are local book festivals. Not a whole lot of sales given the mixed nature of the audience and the abundance of authors, but relationships are established that pave the way for future events. Most important, though… these offer the opportunity to connect directly with the fans. By making a direct connection with them you become more than a name on a cover or page.

As authors we may start out solitary, in a dark room with a computer and a cup of coffee, but to succeed we must venture out. Immerse ourselves in the world and remind them over and over that we are here.

General Publishing Terms

(By no means a comprehensive list, but it is a good selection of common terms. It was compiled for an Anthology seminar I presented at a monthly meeting of The Garden State Horror Writers)

Advance – fee paid to authors upon acceptance of their work drawn against future royalties.

Anthologist – one who creates anthologies from concept to finished manuscript; also called a Packager.

Copyeditor – the person responsible for correcting technical aspects of a manuscript, such as grammar, spelling, and typos.

Copyright – the legal protection declaring your intellectual property yours.

Cover Art – artwork designed, commissioned, or licensed for use on the front cover.

Cover Template – a guide used when typesetting the cover to ensure all relevant data is properly positioned so that no important information is trimmed off during binding.

Critique – offering feedback on a story, making recommendations to strengthen, correct, or improve the writing, noting technical errors and querying points that are unclear. It is up to the author if they utilize the recommendations.

Deadline – the date by which a work must be delivered or a stage in the process completed.

Design – selecting the artistic style, fonts, and layout for the finished book.

Editor – the person responsible for accepting or rejecting submissions and determining the print order of the book; also called a series or project editor.

Edits – corrections or queries the editors require to be addressed in a story before publication.

F&Gs – Stands for folded and gathered signatures (book blocks). The printed text pages of the book sent as a sample of the finished product. Basically a proof copy of the book block, only there is no opportunity to make corrections. However, it does allow you to catch production problems before the printer binds the books.

Flat Fee – payment made to authors in lieu of royalties, generally per word or a set dollar amount.

Galleys – electronic or print copies of the finished manuscript used for the authors and editors to look for any last errors in writing or typesetting so they can be corrected before the book goes to print.

Illustration – black and white line art, halftones, or color images included in the book based on or complementary to the story.

Line Editor – the person responsible for improving the style, plot, and continuity of a story line.

Outline – A bullet list of the major points in the storyline that an author uses to plot out a book. Sometimes a publisher will request to see this before asking for the full manuscript, depending on the publisher.

POD – Print on demand. A digital technology that allows publishers to produce books in low quantity. Often confused with being synonymous with vanity press since they were among the first to make use of the innovation.

Proof – a printed version of the book provided by the printer as a last opportunity to ensure the book is printed properly and there are no major errors.

Proofreader – traditionally, someone who compares typeset pages to the original manuscript looking for errors; in more modern terms, someone who reviews a manuscript for typos but not content.

Proposal – a brief description of the basic story an author intends to submit, also called a synopsis.

Royalties – a percentage paid to the author/contributors for publication of their work. It is generally based upon the net sales price per book sold.

Submission – full-length fiction, or a story offered for potential inclusion in an anthology.

Standard Formatting – double-spaced, first-line indented, standard font (Courier or Times New Roman) with underline representing italics and a tab used for the indent.

Synopsis – A concise description of the plot of the book, something like a book report, only written by the author and submitted, when requested, to the publisher so they can determine if they are interested in seeing the full manuscript. Should not be a tease, but hit on all the major points of the book.

Theme – the unifying topic for a collection.

Typesetting – taking the completed manuscript and formatting it for print.

Work-For-Hire – any art or writing you do as a specific commission for a publisher or corporation for which they retain the copyright or are legally considered the owner of the creative content.

Summing Up

I once saw a squirrel purposely do back flips in an effort to part me from a portion of my lunch. He would flip, stop expectantly, then flip again, gradually getting a little closer. It worked (though I have to admit, he was not much pleased with what I had to offer. He frankly looked a little disgusted that he had gone through such effort.)

I often feel like that squirrel (the flipping part, not the disgust).

As writers, our words seem only to mean half as much until they are read and appreciated by others. Achieving that can require more effort than the writing itself. It really can. But you know what, if you want more than just a book on the shelf, you have to put out that effort. Now I know this can be difficult given that I know more introverted writers than extraverted, but getting out from behind your keyboard and into the public eye is a necessary step to bring attention to your work.

For about nine years now I have been driving up and down the East Coast on the convention circuit and to various author events I have arranged. I can't tell you how many more friends I have, let alone fans of my work due to these efforts. But don't mistake me. This isn't just about waving your work around until someone buys it, author events (well, the successful ones, anyway) go a long way to revitalizing your passion as a writer. At least it does for me. Whether I spend a few minutes or a few hours talking to one person or a room of people about my process and various works I walk away with an energy boost like you wouldn't believe. Some of my best writing is done after such events.

It's about reconnecting with yourself, your passion, and your audience. It is often mistakenly construed that writing is a solitary venture. In truth, the real life of your writing is found in your interactions with others. I get a little scary, I think, when I am talking to a writer just getting started about how and why I did various things in my stories. I have benefited by the reminder of why I love what I do. Sometimes we forget what it's all about… until we see our excitement reflected in the eyes of our readers.

Some authors forget this. Some get caught up in their own importance, distancing themselves from their audience, alienating others in the profession. I strive to remember that the only measure of my success is how connected I am with the reader. The only place prima donnas belong is ballet.

Ty Drago

Ty Drago is a full-time writer and the author of nine published novels, including his five-book *Undertakers* series, the first of which has been optioned for a feature film. *Torq*, a dystopian YA superhero adventure, was released by Swallow's End Publishing in 2018. And his science fiction novel *Dragons* will release through eSpec Books in 2021. Add to these one novelette, myriad short stories and articles, and appearances in two anthologies. He's also the founder, publisher, and managing editor of ALLEGORY (www.allegoryezine.com), a highly successful online magazine that, for more than twenty years, has featured speculative fiction by new and established authors worldwide.

Ty currently just completed The New Americans, a work of historical fiction and a collaborative effort with his father, who passed away in 1992. If that last sentence leaves you with questions, check out his podcast, "Legacy: The Novel Writing Experience," to get the whole story.

He lives in New Jersey with his wife Helene, plus one cat and one dog.

Danielle Ackley-McPhail

An award-winning author, editor, and publisher, Danielle has worked both sides of the publishing industry for longer than she cares to admit. In 2014 she joined forces with husband Mike McPhail and friend Greg Schauer to form her own publishing house, eSpec Books (www.especbooks.com).

Her published works include six novels, *Yesterday's Dreams, Tomorrow's Memories, Today's Promise, The Halfling's Court, The Redcaps' Queen,* and *Baba Ali and the Clockwork Djinn*, written with Day Al-Mohamed. She is also the author of the solo collections *Eternal Wanderings, A Legacy of Stars, Consigned to the Sea, Flash in the Can, Transcendence, Between Darkness and Light, The Fox's Fire, The Kindly One, Dawns a New Day,* and the non-fiction writers' guides *The Literary Handyman, More Tips from the Handyman,* and *Build-A-Book Workshop*. She is the senior editor of the *Bad-Ass Faeries* anthology series, *Gaslight & Grimm, Side of Good/Side of Evil, After Punk,* and *Footprints in the Stars*. Her short stories are included in numerous other anthologies and collections.

In addition to her literary acclaim, she crafts and sells original costume horns under the moniker The Hornie Lady Custom Costume Horns, and homemade flavor-infused candied ginger under the brand of Ginger KICK! at literary conventions, on commission, and wholesale.

Danielle lives in New Jersey with husband and fellow writer, Mike McPhail and two extremely spoiled cats.

www.ingramcontent.com/pod-product-compliance
Lightning Source LLC
Chambersburg PA
CBHW021150080526
44588CB00008B/288